MONEY & POWER

The Secret History

STEVEN S. SADLEIR

Money & Power: The Secret History
by Steven S. Sadleir

ISBN: 146100554X

ISBN-13: 9781461005544

Printed by CreateSpace, an Amazon.com company, for

Self Awareness Institute
668 N. Coast Hwy. #417
Laguna Beach, CA 92651
www.SelfAwareness.com
949-355-3249

Other Books by Steven S. Sadleir

Looking for God: A Seeker's Guide to Religious & Spiritual Groups of the World

Christ Enlightened: The Lost Teachings of Jesus Unveiled

Self-Realization: An Owner-User Manual for Human Beings

"The refusal of King George III to allow the colonies to operate an honest money system, which freed the ordinary man from the clutches of the money manipulators, was probably the prime cause of the revolution."

Benjamin Franklin

Acknowledgements

First I would like to thank Congressman Allard K. Lowenstein, who inspired me to start research for this book over thirty years ago, and to other inspirations: Jesus, Jefferson, Franklin, Monroe, and Paine, as well as Susan B. Anthony, John F. Kennedy, Martin Luther King, Jr., and Ralph Nader—all those who dared because they cared.

I would also like to acknowledge my mentors of business and banking: Professor John D. Russell (Menlo College); Bob Gross (ambassador), Antonio Borges (Stanford University); Professor Revell (University of Wales); Rotary International who paid for my graduate studies as a Rotary Scholar; Mr. Pince (East-West Center); Mr. Brown (Lloyds Bank), Gene Jung (Trinity Capital), and all those with whom I have done business or referred to in this book; and to Representatives Ron Paul, Alan Grayson, Darrell Issa and Dennis Kucinich for speaking up.

My friends Jim Smith, David Smith, Scott Cahoy, Richard Levaitte, Bob Uhl, Mary Houston, Richard Harvey, Janet Dang, and all the students of the Self Awareness Institute who helped create the dialog that developed this book, Crystal and Mark Victor Hansen for great ideas, and to my guru who helped me see the light.

I would also like to acknowledge the men and women of banking and industry, and specifically the contributions of the royalty and wealthy whose knowledge and inspiration developed the economy that we enjoy today despite what improvements are needed. Specifically, I want to acknowledge the contributions of the Windsor, Rothschild, Rockefeller, Bush and other powerful families mentioned in this book who face the public scrutiny but have also made valuable contributions to our world.

Preface

The whole world revolves around money, yet very few people really understand it. The entire world economy operates on a system we call capitalism, yet very few people understand the basis of capitalism, the global banking system, or monetary policy and how it affects our lives. Our ignorance is why we suffer, and why we go through difficult financial times again and again throughout our history. This book is designed to provide you a simplified overview of our monetary system and economy, and give you the insight to make the best decisions. But before I can explain this to you, you need to know where I got my information and how my views were formed. Moreover, I'm not trying to prove that I am right, but rather attempting to get at what is right and invite debate.

During the late 1970s I was going to college at night and selling diamonds and gold as investments during the day. One of my clients was a New York Congressman named Allard K. Lowenstein. Congressman Lowenstein was a civil rights and antiwar activist and was perhaps most famous for leading a movement to open the investigations into both Kennedy assassinations. He was a personal friend of the Kennedy family and believed elements within our own government, including the CIA and the Banking Cartel, were behind both the assignations. During the PBS television show *Firing Line* in 1975, Congressman Lowenstein was interviewed by William F. Buckley Jr. and for the first time the American public was shown the ballistic and forensic evidence that is at odds with the conclusions of the government's own investigation.

When I met Allard, he had told me that he had been warned not to pursue the reopening of the Kennedy investigations or there would be consequences for him and his family. When asked who these people were, he said they were the ones that run our government, the ones who control the money; he told me "Steven, if you want to know who controls the world, just follow the money." That one statement marked a turning point in my life that has ultimately led me, after over thirty years of research and work in this field, to write these words to you.

The following year I enrolled as a junior at Menlo College in Menlo Park, California. Menlo is a small private business school in the San Francisco Bay area. Menlo had a unique student body when I went there to study business, we had princes from the House of Saud, and the sons and daughters with some of the best family names in the United States like Bush, as well as those from the ruling dynasties of Hong Kong, Japan, Iran, and many European countries; my own educational expenses were paid by academic scholarships. As a student I lived in the mansion of a man who lived next to the college and who had worked for the CIA, in public relations, and as an ambassador; he personally knew many presidents and prime ministers, and through him I met leaders in intelligence, government, and business. Menlo had great professors but I think in retrospect I learned more from the conversations with those other young adults, and with the generals, CEOs, senators, and spies than I did from any book.

One morning in class I read in the *Wall Street Journal* that Allard had been shot in the forehead while at his office, and something in me clicked, and I resolved to learn all I could about the Federal Reserve, our banking system, and who controls the world. One of the leading experts in this field at the time, Professor Antonio Borges, happened to be teaching a course titled Money, Credit, and Banking at neighboring Stanford University. The dean of Menlo College gave me special permission to take that course at Stanford University just so I could work with the professor. So, I took his course over the summer along with some Greek philosophy. I further got permission and guidance from Professor Borges, to write a paper on how the Federal Reserve worked for part of my grade as this was what I was particularly interested in learning, and through this research the story began to come together for me.

My revelation about our banking system further inspired me to learn more, and I resolved to dig deeper, and at the same time I was nominated for and ultimately won a Rotary scholarship to study international economics abroad. So, after graduating with a B.Sc. in business administration from Menlo, I was sent to the University of Wales at Bangor, in the United Kingdom, to study financial economics, and specifically international banking. Professor Revell, the head of the Department of Economics, was famous for creating a "balance sheet" for countries and was an authority on global monetary policy. Most of my fellow students in the graduate school already had worked in the central banks of their respective countries: Venezuela, Hong Kong, Iraq, the United Kingdom, etc. Here we learned about the World Bank, the International Monetary Fund (IMF), and how the international banking system works.

The biggest deals made are loans to other countries and syndicated loans, project financing, such as offshore oil drilling, so I wrote my dissertation on *Project Financing, as a Means of Reducing the Country Risk in Foreign Lending*. I provided a model for assessing foreign lending risk, particularly in mineral extraction projects overseas. These syndicated loans involve numerous banks, each participating in projects such as offshore oil drilling or copper-gold mining, and also involve working with the World Bank, IMF, and various governments. It's through the workings of the World Bank and IMF that you begin to see how the world really works, and who controls the world. It was here I learned how a very small group of men actually control the world.

After graduating from the University of Wales with a master's in financial economics, I began working for a United States government agency called the East-West Center in Honolulu, Hawaii. While at this "think tank" I was primarily engaged in feasibility studies on foreign-based mineral extraction projects—cooperative eco-friendly developments in Papua New Guinea, Indonesia, and the Philippines. I also wrote an economic paper on *Commodity Price Stabilization*, as many other nations were threatening to follow the OPEC oil-producing nations in controlling their own natural resources, our government and corporate interests were keen on looking at the possible consequences of price controls on world markets.

From the East-West Center, I moved back to Southern California and began working as the International Economist for Lloyds Bank of California, a wholly owned subsidiary of Lloyds Bank, United Kingdom, which had its office in downtown Los Angeles. At Lloyds, I underwrote our foreign loans, provided economic forecasting for the bank, and was responsible for our compliance with both U.S. and British banking laws, and restructuring our loans to foreign nations and foreign banks. After Lloyds, I became a consultant to other banks, developed commercial real estate, and served as the national sales manager for a mortgage bank.

From international, commercial and mortgage banking I moved into investment banking during the dot-com boom, got my NASD Series 7 and 63 securities licenses, and began working as an underwriter for large investment funds, analyzing markets, industries, and companies. Initially my focus was on equity financing—PIPEs, drips, and convertible instruments, mergers, and venture capital. Essentially we were investing in technology companies and later oil development projects.

It was an exciting time, with myriad new investment opportunities technologies like the Internet, biotech, wind, solar, and cell. Millions and millions of dollars were being invested at blinding speed. At one time I worked for a securities firm that specialized in providing research reports for the oil industry, I also managed funds and had an investment newsletter, and later retired to teach meditation and write. What I learned from it all I would like to share with you—an insider's view of how the world of money and banking work.

This book is condensed and covers a lot of ground very quickly, as if it were a textbook for college students. When you have finished reading this book, you'll know more about how the world really works than most congressmen, businessmen, and educators; this knowledge is necessary if we are to fulfill the dream for which our forefathers fought. Bless you.

Contents

A Brief History of Money   1

Origins of Banking and Capital, Royal Families, the House of Winsor, the House of Rothschild, Corporations, Trusts, and Holding Companies.

History of U.S. Banking   19

Colonial Banking, the Bank of North America, the First Bank of the United States, President Jackson and No Bank, Greenbacks and Prosperity.

American Royalty and Kingdoms   39

The Robber Barons, the House of Morgan, the House of Rockefeller, the Sherman Antitrust Act, the Great Depression, the Federal Reserve Act, and World War I.

Propaganda and The New World Order   65

Bretton Woods, Keynesian versus Monetarist Economics, the Military Industrial Complex, the Council on Foreign

Relations, the Trilateral Commission, the Builderberg Group, the Cabinet, and the New World Order.

Origins of the Central Intelligence Agency, the Assassination of JFK, Multinational Interests, Iran Contra, the House of Bush, and U.S. Global Military Domination.

Oil Politics, Recent Coups, Executive Branch, World Oil, Geo-Political, Project for a New America, Energy, the Enron Loophole, and Cartel Lobbyists.

The IMF, National Debt, Economic Indicators, Consumer Credit and Debt, Globalization, Mega Mergers, the Banking Monopoly, TARP, Derivatives, Equity Markets, the Black Market, Agriculture, and the World's Largest Conglomerates.

Twenty-One Action Steps and Talking Points

A Brief History of Money

In the beginning, man was provided for. The earth gifts humanity with abundant and renewable resources. Land and what it produced was plentiful, but just like in the biblical story of Cain and Able, mankind quickly learned to take ownership, dominate, and covet, and developed jealously, envy, and greed. Mankind's quest has been to learn to live together peacefully and prosper; the devil's been in money, power, and greed.

In ancient days the patriarch or elder was typically the leader, and among brothers the firstborn or strongest became head of the clan. The strongest of the clan heads became kings, dominating villages, townships, and cities. Kings grew in power and wealth by conquering other lands and peoples, acquiring their precious resources and forming empires. As empires grew and as one culture began to dominate another, the very size of the dominion required organization to conduct all the affairs and business of the kings, and their also arose the need to veil the identities of the royalty investing, and so they created corporations and trusts. After the Second World War, these new multinational corporations grew to become bigger and more powerful than the nations that they served, and they began to surpass the power of governments. Today they dominate civilization.

We began seeing cities and civilizations being built around the great rivers. The Egyptian culture flourished along the Nile in Egypt, the Sumerians along the Tigres and Euphrates Rivers in Iraq, and the Harrappan along the Indus River in modern Pakistan/India around ten thousand years ago. Having a year-round water supply enabled them to grow food all year, and expand their capacity to produce food. People settled, and these populations were able to grow and develop specialized skills. Precuneiform script can be found on tablets dating to 3500 BC in Sumer. They were the first culture to develop both a ten-base and six-base numbering system and kept the first written accounts of trading. Thus, the first values, quantities, symbols of exchange, and receipts that were created (according to current knowledge) occurred in this most ancient of civilizations.

Most cultures used bartering for one good for another, or to exchange goods for services such as labor. Values included land, crops, minerals, forest, game, livestock, women, slaves or cheap labor, or ornaments such as shells, feathers, stones, and gems. Precious stones and metals have universally been used as a medium of exchange and store of value—money. The Babylonians were the first to have a system of economics, with rules of debt, legal contracts, and law codes relating to business practices and private property. The code of Hammurabi, the best preserved, dates to 1760 BC, and what we have of the code of Ur-Nammu, from the King of Ur (2050 BC), just before the time of Abraham in the city that Abraham was born.

The shekel, is both a unit of weight and a currency, and was used in Mesopotamia as early as 3000 BC; it referred to a specific weight of barley, which was the main staple in Iraq. The Egyptians used gold bars as a medium of exchange as far back as the fourth millennium, just as the Sumerians had used silver bars before them. The oldest stamped coin dates to 700 BC and is the Greek *drachma* of Aegina, which is known as the *turtle* coin because a turtle is stamped on one side, and some letters and a dolphin are stamped on the other side. Most developed cultures used stamped coin metals as a medium of exchange, and minting of these coins was the prerogative of the king or government; gold, silver, copper and tin were the most common metals used for coins.

In ancient China, merchants would tie their coins to a rope as they were stamped with a hole in the middle. Later those strings of coin would be tallied and left with a trustworthy person who would provide a receipt that could then be traded. As a result of a copper shortage in 960, during the Song Dynasty, paper notes began being traded as a medium of exchange. During the Middle Ages in Italy, and later in Europe generally, in order to facilitate their flourishing wholesale trade in cloth, wine, and tin, goods were supplied to a buyer against a *bill of exchange*, which served as an IOU for payment at a future date. These bills became both a medium of exchange and a store of value; they could be traded for other goods or saved for future use. In England, bills of exchange served as a form of money and credit up to the end of the eighteenth century.

In seventeenth century England, leading goldsmiths who were entrusted with holding the gold of others, would issue receipts for the amount of the gold that they were protecting. These receipts could be traded in for gold or traded as a note that another could trade in for gold. In other words, they were as good as gold. Other economies used silver, and in ancient days notes could be traded for grain. However, knowing that very few of their clients ever needed to redeem their notes for gold, the gold banking cartel began issuing more notes than there was gold, and that's where the trouble begins.

Knowing the goldsmiths were laden with gold, traders approached them for loans. Like the grain bankers before them, goldsmith bankers began issuing gold receipts and then created additional money in the form of demand deposits simply by making numerical entries in their ledgers. In other words, you no longer had to hold the paper notes either; the notes were registered under your name and account at the bank. These London goldsmith bankers—Lombards—were the forerunners of the current banking systems of Europe, then the United States, and eventually the entire world.

Notes not backed by the reserves of another commodity, such as gold, are called *fiat* money (Latin for let it be done), and are given value by decree and by enforcing a law to use it as legal tender. Under the Roman emperor Diocletian and in post-revolutionary France, refusal to use legal tender in favor of another form of payment was punishable by death. Commodity money is backed by an asset such as gold or silver. But all money is only worth what other people perceive its value to be; its strength ultimately lies in the strength of the economy issuing the money.

Banking and Capital

The first banks in ancient times were the temples, where people would store commodities and exchange valuables. Temples would have a patron king, and the two worked together like government and bank. In third century Persia the Sassanid emperors issued sakks, which were basically letters of credit. By the ninth century, Muslim traders were exchanging checks from Bagdad to China, but the first real modern banks developed in Renaissance Italy, particularly in Genoa, Florence, and Venice. In the fourteenth century, the Bardi and Peruzzi families dominated banking in Europe, but the most famous Italian bankers were the Medici, whose business was set up by Giovanni Medici in 1397. The earliest known state deposit bank is the Bank of St. George or Banco di San Giorgio, founded in Genoa, Italy, in 1407.

The Bank of Saint George made use of respected Genoese-Jewish families that were prominent in the late Middle Ages and early Renaissance, especially the particularly well-known family the Ghisolfi. Simeone de Ghisolfi married the reigning princess of Tmutarakan, in the Crimea, and through marriage took possession of the land that became a protectorate of the Genoese consulate throughout much of the fifteenth century. The republic of Genoa ceded its Crimean possession to the Bank of Saint George in 1453. At this point it is important to note two cultural phenomena developing: First, banks were involved in the acquisition of territory and resources and involved in the financing of the wars for territory. Wars create massive debt that makes money for the moneylenders. Moreover, banks not only make loans, they typically have ownership or equity, as well. Now these banks are called merchant banks or investment banks. The second interesting cultural relationship involves the European Jews. Venice is the home of the first Jewish ghetto. At first, the Jews were welcomed in Europe; they brought the knowledge and money for trade, and they have played an integral part in our banking history.

Catholics are prohibited from money changing, and that's what banking is according to the church. So no believers could be bankers or lend money. Moreover, Jews were not typically allowed to own land, so they invested in gold, and some lent money to kings. Most European kings owed money to the money lenders, Jewish or otherwise, and the role of the bankers in our lives and government continued to grow unto this day. The persecution of the Jews during this period was often more a way for a king to get out of paying his debt than a religious matter. However, by the seventeenth century Jewish banking families were an integral part of European growth and trade. Jews have had a long history of trading throughout the

Mediterranean, and using bills of exchange and notes. They were also leading goldsmiths, counting houses, and bankers. So the kings of Europe all had Jewish moneylenders financing their commerce and their wars. This is why you see so many of the old investment banking houses have Jewish German names: Solomon, Kuhn, Loeb, Goldman, Sachs, Warburg, Schiff, and Bauer, which was changed to Rothschild.

Royal Families

The history of Western civilization is one of kings conquering other kings, and the bankers who financed them. Looking more closely at the royal histories of Great Britain and then the United States, it is important to note that the English nation was formed from invading Germanic tribes called Anglo-Saxons beginning around the 5th century AD, who then ruled until the Norman conquest of 1066. The Angles came from Germany, and Saxons came from the Low Countries like the Netherlands these people first conquered and then ruled Great Britain for centuries. But the bloodlines of all the great royal families of Europe have been mixed through many generations of intermarriage. Our history and culture are intertwined with theirs, and so is our struggle.

Royal families continue to this day, including the Belgian, British, Canadian, Spanish, Danish, Dutch, Norwegian, and Swedish, and they are all related. The reigning monarch in England, Queen Elizabeth II, is related by blood to the Germanic Royal Houses of Saxe-Coburg-Gotha, Oldenburg, and Hanover (among others). The British monarchy traces its origins to the early Angles and Scottish Kings. By 1000 the Kingdoms of England and Scotland (and claiming France) had formed Britain, and in the thirteenth century the principality of Wales was also absorbed into Great Britain. In 1603 the Scottish king James VI inherited the English throne as James I, which united the Kingdoms of England and Scotland and Wales under a single monarch.

The Kingdom of Great Britain was formed in 1707 with the merger of the Kingdoms of England and Scotland under the House of Stuart. In 1801 Great Britain merged with the Kingdom of Ireland, forming the United Kingdom of Great Britain and Ireland; then in 1922 80 percent of Ireland left the union and the name was amended to the United Kingdom of Great Britain and Northern Ireland. The **House of Stuart** was founded by Robert II of Scotland and became monarchs of the Kingdom of Scotland in the late fourteenth century.

Nine Stewart monarchs ruled Scotland from 1371 until 1603 when James the VI of Scotland became the claimant to the throne after the **House of Tudor** became extinct (the virgin Queen Elizabeth I had no heir), and **Queen Ann** (1707-1714), the daughter of James II and VII (House of Stuart) and Ann Hyde, the Duchess of York, became the next monarch. Queen Ann married George of Denmark, but their authority was contained during the reformation of the church and of state. There was a populist movement in Great Britain and in 1689 the Parliament passed the English Bill of Rights, which included such new conditions as no royal interference with the law, only the Parliament could tax not royalty, freedom to petition the monarch without fear of retribution, the right for subjects to bear arms, and freedom of speech.

Under the former Tudor dynasty, Great Britain had broken away from the Catholic Church (by edict of King Henry VIII), and the Protestant movement was in full swing, fueled by political motives as much as religious. By 1701 the Parliament of England passed the Act of Settlement, which prohibited monarchs being Catholic. During this time the Parliament was trying to gain power and weaken the monarchy, so after the death of Queen Ann an agreement was made with the Parliament for the Stuarts to drop their claim to the throne in return for access to the English plantations in North America.

Although over fifty Catholics bore closer blood relationship to Anne, the Act of Settlement barred them from succession. George I, the Elector of Hanover in Germany, was Anne's closest non-Catholic relative, and it was he who ascended to the throne beginning the dynasty of the **House of Hanover**, Germany. This served the needs of the new British government, which wanted a king but not one that would actively rule. Sir Robert Walpole, formerly first Lord of the Treasury and a banker, became leader of the Parliament, a position that is now called the prime minister. Walpole was essentially Britain's first prime minister, and now the bankers have the power to create money rather than the royalty.

House of Hanover

King George I (1714-1727) was born in Hanover, Germany, the son of Ernest Augustus the Duke of Brunsewich-Luneburg (from the Albertinian line of the Habsburg family) and Sophia of Hanover (granddaughter of James who united England and Scotland and Princess Palatine of the Rhine). George I married Sophia Dorothea, the only child of the Duke of Brunswick-Luneburg (the Celle line), and she gave birth to George II in Hanover, Germany. George II was the last British monarch to be born outside of Great Britain and the last to lead an army in battle.

King George II (1727-1760) married Caroline of Brandenburg-Ansbach, Germany. She was the daughter of the Margrave of Brandenberg-Ansbach and Princess Eleonore Erdmuthe of Saxe-Eisenach. She gave birth to George III who ruled during the American Revolution; he's mostly German. **George III** (1760-1820) was the grandson of George II, who married

Charlotte of Mecklenburg-Strelitz, electress consort of Hanover, and they had two son's who both became king. First **George IV** was crowned and married Charlotte of Mecklenberg-Strelitz (electress consort of Hanover). After the death of George IV the next son, **William IV,** was crowned and married his brother's wife Queen Charlotte.

The next monarch was **Queen Victoria** (1837-1901), who was the niece of William IV, and the daughter of Prince Edward, who was the Duke of Kent and the fourth son of King George III and Princess Victoria of Saxe-Coburg and Gotha (another kingdom in Germany). Victoria then married Prince Albert who was also from the Royal **House of Saxe-Coburg and Gotha**. In 1917, during the First World War with Germany, the family changed its family name to **Windsor** attributable to anti-German sentiments during the war, and from here on the royal family is considered the House of Windsor. **Edward VII** (1901-1910) was the son and heir of Victoria, and he married Alexandra of Denmark (whose father was Christian IX of Denmark and mother was Louise of Hesse-Cassel, Germany); his heir was George V who was now considered a Windsor.

House of Windsor

George V married Mary of Teck (whose father was Duke Alexander of Wurttemberg and a descendant of the Habsburgs, the ruling family of Austria and Spain); she gave birth to Edward VIII and George VI. **Edward VIII** abdicated the throne to marry American socialite Wallis Simpson (a scandal at the time), and his brother **George VI** (1936-1952) was crowned. King George was married to Elizabeth Bowes-Lyon (whose father was the fourteenth Earl of Strathmore and Kinghorne and Lady Elizabeth Bowes-Lyon of Scottish nobility), their daughter **Elizabeth II** (1952-Present) is the reigning monarch of Britain. Queen Elizabeth married Price Philip of

Greece and Denmark, and they have four children; with Prince Charles as the next heir to the throne.

So the current royal family and primary investor in the Bank of England, as well as in most British industry (throughout the Commonwealth) is a branch of royalty from Germany that has reached into all of Europe. Elizabeth II is related to the queen of the Netherlands and the king of Norway, as well as the former king of Greece, as well as the United States president George Washington. Other lines of the family extend to Scandinavian, Russian, French, and Spanish royal families, and to the corporations and trusts they created together. Royal families, through their agents, have been the primary investors in America and other parts of the former British Empire. That ownership exists to this day, through corporations, trusts, and holding companies. Queen Elizabeth II of Britain and Queen Beatrix of the Netherlands (House of Orange-Nassau) formed the Royal Dutch Shell Oil Company, now just Shell, and British Petroleum (BP) is in partnership with the British government, the royal family, and the king of Norway to develop oil in the North Sea.

Most people don't realize how much our own American royalty is a part of British royalty. Most United States presidents are related to English royalty; according to leading experts, Genealogics and Roglo, Queen Elizabeth II is among the closest living relatives of George Washington, through their descent from Augustus Warner, Burgess of Virginia. The list also includes:

- George Washington to Edward III of England

- Thomas Jefferson to Edward III of England

- James Madison to Edward I of England

- James Monroe to Edward III of England

- John Quincy Adams to Edward III England

- William Henry Harrison to Edward I England

- Benjamin Harrison to Edward I England

- Zachary Taylor to Edward I of England

- Franklin Pierce to Henry I of England

- Rutherford Hays to William I of Scotland

- Grover Cleveland to Edward I of England

- Theodore Roosevelt to James I of Scotland & Edward III of England

- William Taft to Edward III

- Warren Harding to Henry II of England

- Calvin Coolidge to Edward I of England

- Herbert Hoover to Edward III of England

- Franklin Roosevelt to James II of Scotland

- Harry S. Truman to Robert III of Scotland

- Richard Nixon to Henry II of England

- Gerald Ford to Edward I of England

- Jimmy Carter to Henry II of England

- George H.W. Bush to Edward I of England and Robert II of Scotland

- George W. Bush to Edward I of England and Robert II of Scotland

- Barak Obama to Edward I of England and William the Lion of Scotland

The overview of British monarchs is also important in seeing how the influence of German royal houses, with their strong interdependencies with Jewish banking houses, became an integral part of British government and banking, which in turn evolved into American and then world government and banking. For instance, Sampson Gideon (1699-1762) was a prominent Jewish London banker and "adviser of the government" who married royalty and who's son, Sampson Eardley, then became first Baron Eardley. Other prominent Jewish bankers include Claude Montefcore (1858-1938), Edgar Speyer (1862-1932) who financed the British Underground system, and Moses Montefcore (1784-1885) who was knighted by Queen Victoria, received a baronetcy, and was related by marriage to Nathan Rothschild, a leading Jewish Banker from Frankfurt, Germany, who plays a very important role in the story. European banking has been led by Jewish decedents for centuries.

In 1770, Sir William Pitt made a statement that sums this up nicely:

> "There is something behind the throne greater than the king himself."

The House of Rothschild

The House of Rothschild is a German Jewish banking house that has dominated banking around the world. Five lines of the Austrian branch of the family were elevated to Austrian nobility and given hereditary baronies of the Habsburg Empire by Emperor Francis II in 1816. The British branch was also elevated to the British nobility by Queen Victoria. Historians tell us that during the nineteenth century the Rothschild family possessed "by far the largest private fortune in the world, and by far the largest fortune in modern history."

Mayer Amschel Rothschild (1744-1812) was born in Frankfurt, Germany, the son of a prominent banker Amschel Moses Rothschild (originally Bauer). Above the door of their home in Frankfurt hung a red shield coat of arms, and during a time of extreme persecution of Jews, they took the name Rothschild which means red shield. They shared the home with the Schiff family, also prominent Jewish bankers, who were represented by the green shield; the names Schiff and Rothschild are part of the same family banking syndicate. Mayer had five sons who opened offices in the most important banking centers in Europe during a period of rapid expansion, and together they were able to become the dominant financial empire in the world. These five sons were:

> Amschel Mayer Rothschild (1773-1855): Frankfurt
>
> Salomon Mayer Rothschild (1774-1855): Vienna
>
> Nathan Mayer Rothschild (1777-1836): London
>
> Calmann Mayer Rothschild (1788-1855): Naples
>
> Jakob Mayer Rothschild (1792-1868): Paris

During the Napoleonic Wars (1803-1815) Nathan Rothschild gained preeminence in the bullion trade (gold and silver) and was a major investor in government bonds, loans, and securities. From 1813 to 1815 he played an instrumental role in supplying the Duke of Wellington's army with the gold it needed to fight Napoleon; at the same time his other brothers were financing Napoleon. The Rothschild's had a famous network of agents, shippers, and couriers that kept them informed before anyone else. In 1815, Nathan, who was in London, received the news of Napoleon's defeat by Wellington at the Battle of Waterloo, Belgium, a full twenty-four hours before the Parliament or anyone else in London.

With this breaking information on the war, the newspapers of the time reported that Nathan stood on the steps in front of his office where others would wait to see what he would do. Knowing that he always got information first, they wanted to see what he was investing in so they could get in on it. Nathan was seen looking dejected and walked away and started selling assets, reflecting his bearish forecast for the British economy. This led to a massive selling spree that caused the entire market to collapse. The very next day, Nathan was able to buy up those same assets for pennies on the pound and increase his holdings and make obscene profits.

Nathan also knew that the future reduction in government borrowing brought about by peace would create a bounce in British government bonds, so he bought up the government bond market and waited two years until the bonds were on the crest of the short bounce cycle in the market, and then in 1817, sold them for a 40 percent profit, making one of the largest financial "killings" in history. In 1826 he supplied enough gold to the Bank of England to avert a market liquidity crisis, and became one of the Bank's largest investors. This is important to note, for the Bank of England was a private bank with a contract with the British government to issue money and loan to other banks and interests. Those other banks and interests were financing Britain's expansion and trade around the world, including the United States. Rothschild money helped finance the United States through the Bank of England in the beginning and later through various central banks we've had in the United States. British prime minister Lloyd George claimed in 1909 that Lord Nathan Rothschild was the most powerful man in Britain.

The Rothschild banking cartel played an integral part in financing the Industrial Revolution; they financed most of the railways around the world, large projects such as the Suez Canal, and bought up some of the best real estate around the world, i.e., Mayfair, London. They own insurance companies (Royal

& SunAlliance), mining operations (Rio Tinto Group, Societe Le Nickel, and Imerys), and some of the world's best wineries. They invested with De Beers, which has cornered the diamond market and much of the gold market; it financed Cecil Rhodes on his expeditions to Africa and created the colony of Rhodesia. They finance governments and issued bonds on their behalf. The French Rothschild family financed the Franco-Prussian War of the 1870s. The London and Paris families funded the Japanese during the Russo-Japanese War (1907), which helped Japan build into a regional power.

Rothschild is also one of the largest investment banking firms in the world, arranging some of the largest mergers and acquisitions of corporations, new issues, and financial instruments, and typically owning stock in these same companies. The Rothschild family is also believed to be amongst the world's greatest philanthropists, collectors of art, and supporters of the state of Israel, donating the Knesset and Israeli Supreme Court buildings. Other prominent Jewish International banking families include the Bischoffsheims, Pereires, Seligmans, and Lazards.

Corporations, Trusts, and Holding Companies

Corporations are a type of company that offers limited liability to the stockholders, and were originally only established through an act of state, either royal charter or act of Parliament. The oldest commercial corporation is the Stora Kopparberg mining in Falun, Sweden, obtained from King Magnus Eriksson in 1347. Some of the most important early corporations include the Dutch and British East India Companies that opened up trade between Europe and Asia, and the Hudson's Bay Company that played a large part in capitalizing colonialism in North America. Incorporation first became publically available with the passing of the Joint Stock Companies Act of 1856 in the

United Kingdom. Corporations serve to protect the stockholders and keep them anonymous, thus most royalty and wealthy people use them to conduct their business. Most people rarely know who actually runs a corporation, or the interests that own and control them; ownership is hidden and spread out among various trusts, holding companies, and corporations; you won't typically see a family name.

A corporation is overseen by a board of directors who represent the ownership and interests of the owners, and are led by a director or chairman of the board and/or the chief executive officer. Whoever owns the most stock has the most control and can elect seats on the board, thus having more votes and say in the running of the company. The board creates and dictates the policies and governance of the corporation and elects the key officers like the president to implement the policies of the board. The president then manages the daily operations of the company or government. The purpose of a corporation is to maximize the profit for the owners and grow stockholder value; to make as much profit for the stockholders as possible a corporation must work to make as much money from the sale of goods or services, or growth in its assets, and reduce its costs as much as possible without compromising efficiencies. It's all about money.

A trust is a business formed with intent to monopolize business or fix prices, or a board or contract that manages other corporations or people's financial interests. Some of the biggest and best-known trusts include Standard Oil, U.S. Steel, the American Tobacco Company, and J.P. Morgan's International Mercantile Marine Company. Similarly, a cartel is an agreement between competing companies that serve their mutual interests. Holding companies are firms that own other companies' stock, Warren Buffett's Berkshire Hathaway is the largest publicly traded holding company; it owns numerous insurance companies, manufacturing concerns, and retailers. Another form of corporate control are conglomerates, such as, Clear Channel Communications with a massive network of broadcasting channels; they control most of the radio stations in America, through ownership or licensing agreements. In short, they control the air. Corporate stock can also be held in funds that pool other people's money and manage it for them.

At the end of the eighteenth century there were around 300 incorporated companies in the United States, eight were manufacturing and the rest provided public services. New York enacted the first state corporate statute in 1811. In the 1930s more states began enacting corporate law, and the use of incorporation grew at a massive rate. A hundred years ago very few people worked for a corporation, now most people in western society do. Incorporation has spread to China now, and in a matter of a few decades they now have some of the largest corporations in the world, including PetroChina and Industrial and Commercial Bank of China, which vie with ExxonMobil and Microsoft in market capitalization (Financial Times Global 500 September 30, 2010). Corporatization has taken over the world.

The History of United States Banking

From the very beginning the colonies were a commercial venture; colonization is necessary for the cheap labor that is needed to utilize natural resources, to develop, trade, and make a profit. In the late sixteenth century England, Scotland, France, Sweden, Spain, and the Netherlands all began to colonize eastern North America. Many attempts ended in failure. Jamestown, which was founded in May 1607 on the James River in Virginia, was financed by the London Virginia Company and almost failed until tobacco was brought in to cultivate as a cash crop. Spain had the monopoly on tobacco and all of Europe was getting hooked, so the Virginia Company sent Englishman John Rolfe to smuggle the sweeter southern variety of tobacco seeds the Spaniards were trading to Jamestown. This new Orinoco tobacco loved the soil and climate and for the first time the colony thrived; tobacco made the British rich, which led to even more migration and colonization. Hemp, for ropes, was also one of the other major crops that grew the colonial economy, as well as indigo, a dye that accounted for one-third of Americas exports at one time. Later cotton became the major crop; now it's corn.

Some of the major European settlements include New Netherland, a seventeenth-century colonial province of the Republic of the Seven United Netherlands, in what became New York State. This was a joint venture of several royal families. The capital, New Amsterdam, founded in 1625 is located at the southern tip of Manhattan, and was renamed New York after the English captured the city in 1664 and then the whole settlement in 1674. New Sweden was a Swedish colony along the Delaware River Valley from 1638 to 1655. It was centered at Fort Christina, now in Wilmington, Delaware, and it included the current state of Delaware and parts of New Jersey and Pennsylvania. New France was the area explored by Jacques Cartier in 1534 called the Saint Lawrence River. At its peak it extended from Nova Scotia, Canada, to the Great Lakes, and down the Mississippi to the Gulf of Mexico and Louisiana. Most of it was later purchased by the United States from France in the Louisiana Purchase (1803-1804).

Pilgrims from small Protestant sects in England and the Netherlands set up colonies, beginning with the Mayflower landing at Plymouth in 1620. German immigrants came into Pennsylvania, Delaware, New Jersey, and New York, and the Irish settled there, too. By the end of the colonial period there were about 30,000 colonists working for these Royal corporations. After 1700 most immigrants to America arrived as indentured servants, mostly young unmarried men and women seeking a new life; the British shipped over 50,000 convicts to serve as cheap labor to work the tobacco farms. However, the people were treated very poorly, so after Bacon's Rebellion in 1676, the British began importing African slaves instead.

Unlike Europe, where aristocratic families, the bankers and church were in control, the American political culture was open to varying economic, social, and religious interests; it was the Age of Enlightenment, and the citizens wanted to create a better world inspired by the writers Locke, Hume, and later Paine's visions of a more utopian society—an enlightened world. Many were Freemasons, sharing the goal of a universal brotherhood of man. They represented Republicanism, which stressed equal rights, virtuous citizens, and the evils of aristocracy, luxury, and corruption. However, the colonists were still subjects of the king and many were in debt to the companies who had rights to their labor and the nation's natural resources. In addition to a rapid growth in exports of agriculture and manufacturing, the colonies also created a market for British goods in North America, and British exports to America increased 360 percent from 1740 to 1770, creating tremendous wealth.

During the first half of the 1700s the Parliament and king were preoccupied with wars in Europe and let the colonies govern themselves. States issued their own noninterest bearing currency called colonial script, which was printed in the amounts needed for trade. At this time there was no fractionalized lending and no national debt was incurred to create our currency. During this time the colonies thrived like never before, and it got the attention of the king and the bankers who began levying taxes and required the colonies to use only British currency and European banking. A series of measures were taken that changed the course of history, such as:

Currency Act (1764)

Sugar Act (1764)

Stamp Act (1765)

First Quartering Act (1765)

Declaratory Act (1766)

Townshend Revenue Act (1767)

Tea Act (1773)

The Intolerable Acts (1774)

Prohibitory Act (1775)

By the middle of the eighteenth century the whole way of life was changing as each generation nearly doubled the population from 100,000 in 1700 to 200,000 in 1725, and 350,000 by 1750. Land holdings were becoming scarce, so upcoming generations either traveled into the frontiers or went to the cities for work. Taxes placed a heavy burden on the colonists but having their currency eliminated and being forced to use the Bank of England's system of debt caused them to go heavily into debt. United States founding father Benjamin Franklin said in his autobiography:

> The colonies would gladly have borne the little tax on tea and other matters, had it not been that England took away from the colonies their money, which created unemployment and dissatisfaction.

Franklin was against debt-based financing like we use now, and he goes on to make a very important point that is key to our discussion:

> The inability of the colonists to get power to issue their own money permanently out of the hands of George III and the international bankers was the prime reason for the revolutionary war.

After the European system of banking was foisted upon the Americans, Benjamin Franklin said:

> In one year, the conditions were so reversed that an era of prosperity ended, and a depression set in, to such an extent that the streets of the colonies were filled with unemployed.

During the **American Revolution** the colonies began issuing noninterest bearing paper money again at the request of George Washington. The Continental Congress also issued paper money called Continental currency to pay for military expenses, but this time they did not regulate the amount of currency being issued, and it rapidly depreciated. To address these concerns the United States Constitution, ratified in 1788, denied individual states the right to coin and print money, which let it up to the federal government to issue currency.

When Benjamin Franklin was asked to what account did he attribute the colonies great prosperity, before using the Bank of England and their debt based central banking, he replied:

> That is simple. In the Colonies we issue our own money. It's called Colonial Script. We issue it in proper proportion to the demands of trade and industry to make the products pass easily from the producers to the consumers. In this manner, creating for ourselves our own paper money, we control its purchasing power, and we have no interest to pay to no one.

The First Central Banks in America

In 1782 the **Bank of North America**, a private bank, was charted by the Congress at the urging of Robert Morris, Alexander Hamilton, and Thomas Wiling. Robert Morris had served an apprenticeship with the Philadelphia banker and merchant Charles Wiling (Banking family from Bristol, England), and later created Wiling, Morris, & Company, which imported and sold slaves. Morris rose to become superintendent of finance of the United States from 1781 to 1784. In 1781 the United States was in a crisis, the Treasury was $25 million in debt because of English debt-based banking, and then public credit collapsed as the bankers had withdrawn money from the economy. Three days later Morris proposed the establishment of a central bank. This bank was funded in part through loans Morris had obtained from the international bankers in France in 1781. The initial role of the bank was to finance the war against Britain, but the bank was created behind closed doors and when the public found out they were angry. The Bank of North America was very much opposed by Thomas Jefferson and the Jeffersonian camp, so in 1785 when Thomas Jefferson became president the bank's charter was not renewed, and the colonies began to prosper again.

Six years later Alexander Hamilton, who had become secretary of the treasury, proposed another European type central bank called the **First Bank of the United States**, which had essentially the same charter as the Bank of North America, which preceded it. Governor Morris, who was head of the committee for the Constitution, wrote in a letter to James Madison commenting on the proposed banking system in July 1787:

> The rich will strive to establish their dominion and enslave the rest. They always did and always will.

Alexander Hamilton was a student of the French finance minister Jacques Necker. Necker apprenticed in 1747 at the bank of Isaac Vernet, a prominent Jewish banker in Paris and partner with the Rothschild syndicate; Hamilton also studied with Britain's chancellor of the exchequer (treasurer) Robert Walpole. Under Walpole the restrictions on banking were lifted and a wave of speculation led to another credit crises.

The South Sea Bubble in 1720 was the result of debt created for the costs of the War of the Spanish Succession, which caused the bankers to restrict the money supply again and the economy began to collapse. The Bank of England was able to receive financial assistance from the Rothschild cartel, which ended up gaining more ownership and control of the Bank of England, which in turn was lobbying for a central bank in America. The same year the First Bank of the United States opened, Amshell Rothschild was quoted as saying:

> Give me issue and control of a nation's money, and I care not who writes the laws.

Walpole worked closely with the Rothschilds to restructure the debt of the Bank of England, and this alliance between bankers and government has continued to this day. In this same year a private central bank, the First Bank of the United States, began controlling the issuance of the nation's currency. This plan was put forward by Hamilton at the first session of the first Congress to fund the Bank of the United States through the sale of $10 million of stock, where the United States government put up $2 million, and the rest would be placed by private investors, including bankers from London and France. However, the United States government did not have the $2 million, so they had to borrow much of the money to capitalize the bank. Much of the private investment came from British and French bankers, which at this time were both intricately involved with the Rothschild cartel.

Moreover, the Congress was concerned about the accumulation of interest on the debt, so Hamilton repeatedly and strongly promoted the idea of increasing the duty on imported spirits and raising the excise tax on domestically distilled spirits. The primary choice of spirit for Americans at the time was hard cider or whiskey. This idea was violently opposed by the American people and led to the Whiskey Rebellions from 1791-1794, where armed resistance to tax collectors broke out in western Pennsylvania. It was these events that led to the creation of two political parties: Jefferson's Republican Party, which were against central banking, and Hamilton's Federalist Party, which supported it.

When Jefferson was elected the third president, after John Adams, in 1801, he repealed the whiskey tax and set out to destroy the central bank. Americans were concerned that a central bank would result in a "money monopoly" increasing interest rates and harming the very business interests it was supposed to protect, and it was, so the bank's charter was not renewed and the United States began issuing its own currency again, and it prospered. In 1811 the bank's charter expired, however, this usurpation of the European moneylenders was a contributing cause of the British invasion and the War of 1812. It was a war of the classes—the rich and the common man. In the words of Thomas Jefferson:

> If the American people ever allow the banks to control the issuance of their currency the banks and corporations that grow up around them will deprive the people of their property, until their children wake up homeless on the continent their fathers conquered.

One of our most important founding fathers makes it very clear he, and they collectively, were against the central banking system we have now. Jefferson had studied the European central banking system and was passionately against it. In a letter to Secretary of the Treasury Albert Callatin in 1802, Thomas Jefferson wrote:

> I believe that banking institutions are more dangerous to our liberties than standing armies. If the American people ever allow private banks to control the issue of their currency, first by inflation and then by deflation, the banks and corporations that grow up around those banks will deprive the people of all property.

Jefferson then went further to say:

> The issuing power should be taken from the banks and restored to the people to whom it properly belongs.

Knowing he was setting a precedent as the first president of the United States, George Washington was hesitant about signing the "bank bill" into law. Washington asked for a written opinion from all his cabinet members and most particularly from Hamilton. The first attorney general, Edmund Randolph from Virginia, felt the bill was unconstitutional. Jefferson, serving as secretary of state at the time, also agreed that Hamilton's proposal was against the spirit and letter of the Constitution. One of the comments against Jefferson:

> [I]n a masterpiece of legal obfuscation, well calculated to confuse the president, he [Jefferson] asserted the bank bill violated the laws of mortmain, alienage, forfeiture and escheat, distribution and monopoly. Washington, overwhelmed by the arguments...sent Hamilton copies of Randolf's and Jefferson's opinion...inviting Hamilton in effect to defend the bank if he could.

James Madison was also very much against the formation of a central bank. He called central bankers the money changers, in a clear biblical reference to the time Jesus Christ expressed disgust and anger by turning over the tables of the money changers (bankers) who worked at the temple in Jerusalem. Madison said:

> History records that the moneychangers have used every form of abuse, intrigue, deceit, and violent means possible to maintain their control over their governments by controlling the money and its issuance.

Washington reluctantly signed the bank bill into effect in 1791 and the United States went rapidly into debt on the loans it was now forced to make, and so the Congress did not renew the banks charter when it expired in 1811. In response to the effects of the First Bank, Thomas Jefferson said:

> I wish it were possible to obtain a single amendment to our Constitution taking from the federal government their power of borrowing.

After the charter for the First Bank of the United States expired, Stephen Girard purchased most of its stock, building, and furnishings in Philadelphia and opened his own bank, Girard Bank. **Girard's Bank** was the principal source of government credit during the War of 1812, underwriting 95 percent of the government debt, essentially serving as his own private bank using European money. Girard became one of the richest men in America from this.

Girard also became a large stockholder and director of the **Second Bank of the United States**. Girard was a ship captain from France who was financed by the French Rothschild cartel, who presumably put up the capital for his bank. The Girard Bank merged with the Mellon Bank in 1983 and later became a part of Citizens Bank. According to Michael Klepper and Robert Gunther in their book *The Wealthy 100*, Girard was the fourth-wealthiest American of all time, behind John D. Rockefeller, Cornelius Vanderbilt, and John Jacob Astor.

So we can see that George Washington, Thomas Jefferson, Benjamin Franklin, and James Madison, along with most of the other founding fathers, were all against the formation of a central bank, privately held, that issued the nation's money and charged interest; but the people who did want it had lots of money behind them to keep pushing to establish one, and so they kept lobbying. The only people for it were the bankers, and those who receive money from bankers.

Six years later the same people who pushed for the First Bank of the United States proposed a Second Bank of the United States. Although the stockholders remain a secret, we know at least a third of the investors were foreigners; we also know that Girard was a major investor, and his money came from the International Bankers. According to American historian Arthur Schlesinger, the conflict over having a central bank was between the wealthy Whigs and the working-class democrats, who ultimately always end up paying the debt being created. The growth of vast wealth for the few was paid by the working class in taxes and inflation. During this time the economy suffered because of the massive debt being created from the interest on government loans, so like the First Bank of the United States the bank failed to get its charter renewed; it existed for five more years as an ordinary bank before going bankrupt in 1841.

Communism

In 1848 revolutionary German political theorist Karl Marx and Friedrich Engels wrote one of the world's most powerful political manuscripts called *The Communist Manifesto*, which outlines the precepts of the communist philosophy. Marx's premise is that there is a class struggle between the wealthy and the working class, and views capitalism as a means of subjugating the laboring class; the struggle for the working class to be represented fairly in government is called socialism. Today that term refers to broader powers of government and entitlements to taxpayers. Marx's theories tried to control the economy through the state, and the fifth plank of his *Communist Manifesto* is for the centralization of credit in the hands of the state, by means of a central bank that has exclusive monopoly power over the creation of currency and credit.

The monopoly of money is a communist idea, and the free market is totally against such monopolies. Centralized and unquestioned control is also a communist idea. Americans have always resisted monopolies, especially over money and credit; one president after another is fighting against it.

President Jackson and No Bank

Andrew Jackson (1767-1845), the seventh president of the United States, was the last president to have fought in the Revolutionary War (at thirteen he served as a courier), and became famous for commanding the attack against the British army in the Battle of New Orleans during the War of 1812 and winning. Known as Old Hickory, Jackson was a fighter, in addition to fighting the Revolutionary War, and the War of 1812 and again in the First Seminole War, fighting the Seminole and Creek Indians in Georgia and Spanish Florida, and then in the Congress as a senator for the state of Tennessee. But his biggest battle, by his own account, was to put an end to the European styled central bank in America. Jackson was determined to kill the bank, stating:

> More than eight million of the stock of this bank are held by foreigners...Is there no danger to our liberty and independence in a bank that in its nature has so little to bind it to our country?

Jackson ran for president with the slogan Jackson and no bank. After being elected he did not renew the charter for the bank, and America experienced one of its most prosperous eras. In 1835, Jackson managed to reduce the federal debt to only $33,733.05, the lowest it had been since 1791. By implementing a tariff and term limits on elected officials he remains the only president to pay off the national debt, he also campaigned to abolish the Electoral College, which is politically manipulated, in favor of a one person, one vote system.

In President Jackson's veto message he states his reasons for abolishing the central bank:

> It concentrated the nation's financial strength in a single institution
>
> It exposed the government to control by foreign interests
>
> It served mainly to make the rich richer
>
> It exercised too much control over members of Congress
>
> It favored northeastern states over southern and western states
>
> A few select families controlled it.

It had a long history of instigating wars between nations, forcing them to borrow funding to pay for them.

After Jackson's reelection he ordered the nation's gold reserves to be moved from the Second Bank of the United States (the central bank) to the primary state banks. First he ordered Louis McLane, secretary of the treasury, to move the gold but McLane refused because he was a part of the bank syndicate. So he fired McLane and ordered the assistant secretary of the treasury who became Treasury Secretary, William J. Duane, who also refused and was subsequently fired, and so Jackson hired Roger B. Taney for the job. Taney finally complied. Two bankers refused the president of the United States—that's how powerful the banking syndicate was even then. The Second Bank of the United States was run by Nicholas Biddle at that time, and he fought hard to keep his bank. He opposed Jackson and threatened a depression if the bank was not rechartered, stating:

> If this worthy president thinks that because he has scalped Indians and imprisoned judges he is to have his way with the bank he is mistaken.

In order to put pressure on the Congress to keep control of the bank and U.S. money supply, the bank restricted the money supply and made threats causing the Panic of 1837, and then Biddle even had the audacity to refuse to show the accounting books of the Central Bank to the Congress. In Biddle's own words:

> Nothing but widespread suffering will produce any effect on Congress...Our only safety is in pursuing a steady course of firm restriction—and I have no doubt that such a course will ultimately lead to restoration of the currency and recharter of the bank.

Three days after Jackson's veto to end the bank, an assassination attempt was made on the president. Jackson, of course, believed the bankers were behind the attempt and took much pleasure in knowing that they failed. They never caught the conspirators. Biddle was arrested and charged with fraud but was later acquitted. When Andrew Jackson was asked in the later years of his life what his most significant accomplishment was, he replied, "I killed the bank."

The period following the fall of the Second Bank of the United States is referred to as the **Free Banking Era** (1837-1862). In this period, only state-chartered banks existed, and they could issue bank notes against specie (gold and silver coins), and they regulated their own reserve requirements, interest rates, and capital ratios. The real value of these bank bills was often lower than its face value, with the financial strength of the bank determined the size of the discount. By 1797 there were twenty-four chartered banks in the United States. This unregulated market led to what was called **Wildcat Banking,** which created inflation, too many banks were creating too many notes, the currency wasn't being regulated. To help stabilize the banking industry in New York, the banks came together to create a form of insurance they called the New York Safety Fund, which provided deposit insurance for member banks.

The years after Jackson and before the Civil War were boom years for the United States, although the banks and government were having difficulties managing inflation, they prospered, and employment was high. The European bankers and royalty were concerned about the prosperity of the United States and the power that comes with it, so they plotted to divide and conquer our nation, and take control of the currency and commerce. Otto von Bismark (1815-1898) was the prime minister of Prussia; he unified the many kingdoms of Germany into the German Empire in 1871, becoming its first chancellor. Bismark sat in the central seat of European power at the time. Explaining the balance of power going on at the time he said:

The division of the United States into the federations of equal force was decided long before the Civil War by the high financial powers of Europe. These bankers were afraid that the United States, if they remained as one block, and as one nation, would attain economic and financial independence, which would upset their financial domination over the world.

Greenbacks

Contrary to popular belief, the American Civil War (1861-1865) was not fought over slavery; it was fought over trade and banking. Only after the Civil War was in full swing did Lincoln decide to emancipate the slaves. The Civil War was expensive, so Lincoln went to the banks to seek loans to pay for government expenditures and was offered rates of interest at 24 to 36 percent. He sought financial advice from his trusted adviser Colonel Dick Taylor who told Lincoln:

> Why, Lincoln, that's easy. Just get Congress to pass a bill authorizing the printing of full legal tender treasury notes...Pay your solders with them and go ahead and win your war with them, also.

The noninterest bearing notes printed by the Treasury are still backed by the strength of the national economy and its gold reserves, but if the country simply issues its own notes it does not have to be charged or pay interest—there is no interest on the national debt because there is no debt; if there is too much money in circulation creating inflation, you simply take some money out of circulation. If the economy slows down, you simply make money more available. You manage the flow of currency for steady growth. The money added into the economy for jobs for the people, not the bankers, increases the tax base, revenues, and profits. It's a lever, and whoever controls the lever controls the country—at least according to most United States presidents.

So Lincoln took control, and in 1862-1863 the United States Treasury began issuing its own currency at no interest to the government; they were printed green on the back—hence the name greenbacks. The economy prospered, at least in the North, but inflation ran high. During this period of rapid economic expansion the economy was not based on the fractionalized, debt-based, capitalism—European banking—it was using the American-based system of the U.S. Treasury creating the currency as it was needed. America also freed itself from European exploitation by limited free trade and providing tariffs to protect American industry and jobs. In 1900 the president explained his position quite clearly:

> Thirty years of protection has brought us to the first rank in agriculture, mining, and manufacturing development, we lead all nations in these three great departments of industry. We outstrip even the United Kingdom which had centuries start of us, her a fiscal policy for fifty years has been of free trade rather than a tariff policy of the democrats, ours for thirty one years the protective policy of the Republicans. Try by any test measure by any standard we lead all the rest of the world. Protection has vindicated itself.

The European banking industry was lobbying hard to create a European-based central bank in America. There was also continued pressure for the banks to take control of the currency again, so the Congress passed the **National Banking Act of 1863** to create a system of national banks with greater reserve requirements, create a uniform national currency, and now, the national banks were required to back up their notes with Treasury securities, creating national debt. Thus, the European debt-based system was reintroduced. By 1865, there were already 1,500 national banks in America, and they were often capitalized with European banking money and the government lost control of the economy again.

United States secretary of the treasury Salmon P. Chase, who originally was for the bank lamented in 1865:

> My agency, in promoting the passage of the National Banking Act was the greatest mistake of my life. It has built a monopoly which affects every interest in the country.

Lincoln and Chase were going to try to change the system again and take control over the currency when President Lincoln was assassinated by John Wilkes Booth.

European newspapers at the time claimed that Booth was hired by the international bankers who didn't want the greenbacks to come back and take their business away, but that claim was never proven.

The banks then again pulled money out of circulation and America sank into another depression.

To gain an idea of how it works look at the following table:

Post Civil War Depression

Year	Dollars in Circulation	Per Capita
1866	$1.8 Billion	$50.46
1867	$1.3 Billion	$44.00

The banks call in two-thirds of all the money in circulation and stopped making loans driving the economy into a depression.

1876	$0.6 Billion	$14.60
1886	$0.4 Billion	$6.67 *

Source Wikipedia

James A. Garfield, America's twentieth president, wanted to take the issuance of money away from the bankers again and return to the Treasury notes. In 1881 he wrote:

> Whoever controls the volume of money in any country is absolute master of all industry and commerce... And when you realize that the entire system is so easily controlled, one way or another, by a few powerful men at the top, you will not have to be told how periods of inflation and depression originate.

He was assassinated just a few months after making this statement.

Great Britain's central bank, the Bank of England, was the center of world banking at this time, and Sir Josiah Stamp, a Baron and former director of the Bank of England, explained the world power paradigm as follows:

> The bankers own the earth, take it away from them, but leave them the power to create money, and with the flick of a pen they will create enough money to buy it back again. However, take away from them the power to create money, and all the great fortune like that will disappear and they ought to disappear, for this world would be a happier and better world to live in. But if you wish to remain slaves of bankers and pay the cost of your own slavery, let them continue to create money.

In a statement by the American Bankers Association in 1894, just a few years before the Great Depression, this industry made perfectly clear its intention to create a depression, as printed in the Congressional Record of April 29, 1913 states in response to regulation of the industry:

On September 1, 1894 we will not renew our loans under any consideration. On September 1st we will demand our money...We will foreclose and become mortgagees in possession. We can take two-thirds of the farms west of the Mississippi, and thousands east of the Mississippi, at our own price...Then the farmers will become tenants as in England.

Now, remember this statement when we come to the discussion on the Great Depression, which is next, but first you need to know the key players—American royalty.

American Royalty and Kingdoms

The eighteenth and nineteenth centuries were a period of massive change in agriculture, manufacturing, mining, and transportation; then technology profoundly changed the socioeconomic and cultural landscape of Western civilization. In the two centuries beginning in 1800 the world's average per capita income increased over tenfold, while the world's population increased sixfold. A giant working class developed, and the cartels of Europe conquered the world economically.

In the later part of the eighteenth century the draft-animal-based economy transitioned to a machine-based manufacturing economy; mechanization was affecting the textile industry and the iron and steel industries; trade was being expanded by the introduction of canals, improved roads and railways; the introduction of steam power, engines, and then oil forged the Industrial Revolution, and it was all financed and led by a very small group of people.

European Bankers, going through United States agents like the J.P. Morgan Banking syndicate, financed America's growth. These first multimillionaires became America's royalty; corporations were their kingdoms. While a new class of ultrawealthy was being born, much of the working class of America felt that that wealth was being created through their blood, sweat, and tears so the people called these industrialists Robber Barons. The Industrial Revolution was also a class war, and corporations became the invisible boss so many Americans went to work for.

The Robber Barons became the board of directors for the American government. Some of the better-known American Barons and their industries include:

John D. Rockefeller - oil

Andrew Carnegie - steel

Henry Clay Frick - steel

John Warne Gates - steel

Edward Henry Harriman - railroads

Cornelius Vanderbilt - railroads

Henry Morrison Flagler - railroads

Leland Stanford - railroads

Charles Crocker - railroads

Jay Gould - railroads

J.P. Morgan - banking

Jay Cooke - banking

Daniel Drew - banking

James Fisk - banking

John Jacob Astor - real estate

James Buchanan Duke - tobacco

From this list we see the barons focused on railroads, steel, oil, and finance. Building railroads across America was very capital intensive, so as an inducement to make the investment to build them, our government granted the railroad corporations the land around the railway lines, typically five miles either side of the track. As development occurred closest to the main transportation lines, the railroad interests soon had some of the best real estate in the country as those land values went up with the development of new cities over time.

New steel-making techniques, new canals to transport raw materials and cheap hydroelectric energy from the Allegheny, Monongahela, and Ohio Rivers made Carnegie and other steel magnates and their investors inconceivably wealthy as they met America's need for steel in skyscrapers, steamships, and all the machines being produced. They profited from the mad dash to cover the nation (and world) with railroads and build steam ships to cross oceans while John D. Rockefeller made history with his Standard Oil monopoly. Underlying and managing it all were the financiers and bankers, and in the Industrial Revolution banking included both loans with interest and equity ownership and control of those corporations and trusts they were investing in or creating.

These barons not only helped grow the economy, they built the United States into the world's greatest superpower economy, but they also did it with American labor and with the people's natural resources. This give and take between the 1 percent and the rest of the world makes or breaks a country or society. For now, those who have the gold rule, and those golden investors were in Europe using U.S. agents like the Morgan cartel.

House of Morgan

J.P. Morgan & Company was an commercial and investment banking corporation founded by J.P. Morgan, the result of the world's two largest banking institutions merging: J.P. Morgan Chase and Morgan Stanley. In 2000, J.P. Morgan was acquired by the Chase Manhattan Bank, a Rockefeller holding, to form J.P. Morgan Chase & Co, one of the world's largest banking syndicates. The company began in 1854 when J.P.'s father, Janius S. Morgan joined a London-based banking syndicate headed by George Peabody (who married Elisha Riggs of the Riggs Bank). Peabody had established a banking house in London in 1835, and he and Janus Morgan were investing European money into American investments such as railroads, steel, oil, armaments, and banking. Janius Morgan was an agent for both the Bank of England and Nathan Rothschild, whose banking cartel already dominated international banking in Europe and around the world. Royal European investors used the Morgan enterprise as their feet on the street in America to find good investments. Janius Morgan then placed his son, J.P. Morgan, in charge of the American office, most of the money Morgan yielded wasn't his—it was European royalty's.

The other important partner to know is William Wilson Corcoran a prominent banker who was, in turn, partners with George Washington Riggs who founded what is now the PNC Bank and Riggs Bank (in which the Bush family also have interests). In 1871 J.P. Morgan joined Philadelphia banker Anthony J. Drexel of what would become Drexel Burnham Lambert in building the world's largest banking cartel. J.P. Morgan & Company, using European money, financed most of the major railroads and was Edward Harry Harriman's primary investor, as well as John D. Rockefeller's and Andrew Carnegie. It was Morgan who was behind consolidating America's steel companies to form the conglomerate United States Steel; in 1901 it controlled two-thirds of all steel production and later acquired

Marathon Oil. Morgan also financed the consolidation of oil companies for Rockefeller to form the Standard Oil Company, which controlled over 80 percent of the world's oil.

After Janius died, J.P. Morgan took on Edward Grenfeld as a partner. Grenfeld had been director of the Bank of England and brought in additional financial partners from Europe, and Morgan's cartel started buying up other banking houses to consolidate power including Manufacturers Hanover, Chase Manhattan, Hambrecht and Quist, Robert Fleming & Company, and the Beacon Group now CCMP, all icons of American finance and banking. Through these acquisitions Morgan also had interests in the Chemical Bank, One Equity Partners, Citigroup, Credit Suisse First Boston, Standard Chartered Bank (UK), Jardine Fleming (Hong Kong), Apple Computer, Genentech, Adobe Systems, Netscape, Amazon, Overstock, Bank One, Bear Stearns, Washington Mutual, Wells Fargo, Bank of America, Union Carbide, Chemical Bank, and many others. Morgan also created a partnership with the Bank of England to become the sole underwriter for war bonds for the United Kingdom and France during WWII—all money raised to fight Adolph Hitler in World War II.

House of Rockefeller

John Davison Rockefeller founded the Standard Oil Company in 1870. John was born in Richford, New York, in 1839 the son of a traveling salesman, Big Bill, who encouraged John to learn how to sell. Rockefeller started his business career as a book-keeper, and was known to be particularly good at calculating transportation costs, a talent that served him well when he got into the oil business. In 1859 he first went into the produce business with Maurice Clark, and then in 1863 they went in together to build an oil refinery in Cleveland's industrial district called "the Flats." Whale oil had become expensive and oil was starting to be used as a replacement for lighting fuel (before electricity), and then, of course, later it was used as the fuel for internal combustion engines and motor transportation.

In 1865 Rockefeller bought out the Clark brothers' refinery for $72,500 at an auction and said, "It was the day that determined my career." In 1866 David's brother William built another refinery in Cleveland and made John a partner. In 1867 he formed Rockefeller, Andrews (a chemist), & Flagler (a railroad tycoon) to build what became the largest refinery in the world. By the end of the Civil War, Cleveland was one of the five main refining centers in the United States, and with the financial help of Morgan he expanded his operations into Pittsburgh and Philadelphia, Pennsylvania, and New York. In 1870 Rockefeller consolidated his refineries into the Standard Oil Company, which rapidly became the largest oil company in the world.

Railroads were fighting fiercely for traffic in an attempt to create a cartel to control freight rates formed the South Improvement Company with Rockefeller's Standard Oil who needed the railroads to transport the oil. By Rockefeller agreeing to use their railroads in high volume, and being financed by Morgan, who also financed the railroads, they offered Rockefeller rebates up to 50 percent, this cut Rockefellers transportation costs and gave him a substantial competitive advantage over the other refiners who had to pay full fair. Thus, Rockefeller was able to drive all the other refiners out of business whereupon he bought them up for pennies on the dollar and took complete control of the industry. By 1872 Standard Oil had absorbed twenty-two of its twenty-six Cleveland competitors. Today the House of Rockefeller still controls over 80 percent of the world's oil refining.

Rockefeller quickly became the richest man in America, and to consolidate his holding in multiple states his lawyers created a innovative form of corporation called a trust, with forty-one companies under its control. This new enterprise included over 20,000 domestic wells, 4,000 miles of pipeline, 5,000 tank cars, and 100,000 employees. During the 1880s the Paris Rothschild's cartel began financing Rockefeller, and they began expanding into other states and countries such as Russia, Burma, and Java (Indonesia), and expanded into natural gas and then gasoline for automobiles. In the 1890s Rockefeller expanded into iron ore and ore transportation, and then into many other industries, mining copper and aluminum, railroads and banking; Nelson Rockefeller was CEO of the Chase Manhattan Bank for twenty years.

The Sherman Antitrust Act

As the Standard Oil monopoly grew in power, and as the price of oil went through the roof, President Theodore Roosevelt led an attack on the trusts and the Congress enacted the Sherman Antitrust Act in 1890 to break up the monopoly and foster competition in the industry. As explained by the United States Supreme Court in *Spectrum Sports, Inc.* v. *McQuillan*:

> The purpose of the [Sherman] Act is not to protect businesses from the workings of the market; it is to protect the public from the failure of the market. The law directs itself not against conduct which is competitive, even severely so, but against conduct which unfairly tends to destroy competition itself.

There are two important sections of the Sherman Antitrust Act that summarize the intention of the law:

Section 1: "Every contract, combination in the form of trust or otherwise, or conspiracy, in restraint of trade or commerce among the several States, or with foreign nations, is declared to be illegal."

Section 2: "Every person who shall monopolize, or attempt to monopolize, or combine or conspire with any other person or persons, to monopolize any part of the trade or commerce among the several states, or with foreign nations, shall be deemed guilty of a felony..."

The United States then passed the **Clayton Antitrust Act** in 1914 to end "price discrimination between purchasers, exclusive dealings agreements, tying arrangements and mergers and acquisitions that reduce competition." The court ruled that the trust was an illegal monopoly and ordered that Standard Oil be broken up into thirty-four new companies, the principal ones we know are Continental Oil or Conoco, now ConocoPhilips; Standard of Indiana, which became Amoco, now a part of British Petroleum or BP; Standard of California, which became Chevron; Standard of New Jersey, which became Esso and later Exxon, and is now part of ExxonMobil; Standard of New York, which became Mobil (ExxonMobil); Standard Oil of Ohio, which became Sohio, now also a part of BP; Penn State Oil, which with merged with George Bush's Zappatta Oil to become Pennzoil. However, the Rockefellers were still able to own their controlling interests in each company and simply had officers in his Standard Oil Company manage each of the new entities, and this made him even richer; it had a similar effect as a stock split, and increased power of the conglomerate.

During this same period President Theodore Roosevelt worked diligently to curb the power of the cartels and trusts that were running the country. One of his first notable acts as president was to deliver a 20,000-word address to Congress asking it to curb the power of large corporations and bankers. In a public address the president stated:

> These International bankers and Rockefeller Standard Oil interests control the majority of newspapers and the columns of those papers to club into submission or drive out of public office officials who refuse to do the

bidding of the powerful corrupt cliques which compose the invisible government.

In Theodore Roosevelt's Bull Moose Party speech that called for vigorous government intervention to protect the people from self-serving corporate interests, he stated:

> To destroy this invisible government, to dissolve the unholy alliance between corrupt business and corrupt politics is the first task of the statesmanship of the day.

In order to address the issues of these giant trusts and banking concerns, President Roosevelt appointed a **National Banking Commission**. Leading the commission was Senator Nelson Aldridge from Rhode Island, whose daughter married John D. Rockefeller and had five sons: John, Nelson, Lawrence, Winthrop, and David. Senator Aldridge represented the Rockefellers and the banking cartel, and after the commission was formed, he left to live in Europe for two years to learn the European banking system and attain capitalization for the new central bank they were planning to form. **Henry Davison**, a German central banking émigré and senior partner with J.P. Morgan, was another founder of the Federal Reserve, as well as **Samuel Bush**, grandfather of American President George H.W. Bush.

The J. Henry Schroder Bank and Trust, one of the largest trusts and asset managers in Great Britain and for the Royal family, is an investor of the Federal Reserve; J. Henry Schroder Bank and Trust is listed in *Standard & Poors* as a subsidiary of Schroders Ltd. of London. Another investor in the Federal Reserve is the National Bank of North America, which is a subsidiary of one of London's largest banks the National Westminster Bank. Still another, the European American Bank is a subsidiary of European American Bank, Bahamas, Ltd., whose directors are all from European banking groups.

Another key player in the formation of America's central bank was **Paul Warburg**, who's family founded M.M. Warburg &

Co. (Hamburg, Germany, in 1798), S.G. Warburg (London in 1946), and Warburg Pincus in New York in 1938. Paul Warburg became a partner of **Kuhn, Loeb and Company**, which was founded by two prominent Jewish bankers from Germany, Abraham Kuhn and Solomon Loeb. **Jacob Schiff** (Shift), 1847-1920) was born in the Rothschild house in Frankfurt, Germany, emigrated to the United States, married Therese Loeb, the daughter of Solomon Loeb and founder of Kuhn, Loeb and Co. Schiff became senior partner and chief executive officer of the Kuhn, Loeb banking syndicate; Schiff was also the first to propose the central bank and capitalize the Federal Reserve. All these families are intermarried and have shared business interests, often investing together in syndicates. The Rothschild—the Red Shield—are partners with the Schiff—the Green Shield—with common ancestors and corporations and business interests; they form a European syndicate, now a global syndicate or cartel.

When Senator Aldridge returned with his instructions, he met with other members of the European syndicate in secret in J.P. Morgan's own hotel on Jekyll Island, Georgia. Of those attending, two represent Morgan's interests, two represent Rockefeller interests, two are German central bankers, and all of them receive money from the Rothschild syndicate. Jacob Schiff gave a speech in 1906 that began the push for central banking in the United States—the debt based fractional reserve banking used in Europe and then the United States— creating fear, and suggesting the need for a central bank, saying:

> [The] country needed money to prevent the next crisis.

Kuhn and Loeb played an integral part in financing America's railroad lines and growth companies including Western Union and Westinghouse. Warburg was getting paid half a million dollars a year to lobby the American congress to create a central bank. Schiff also became director of the National City Bank of New York, Equitable Life Assurance, Wells Fargo Bank, Union

Pacific Railroad, and other interests with E.H. Harriman. In 1907 the *New York Times Annual Financial Review* published the first official plan from Warburg for a central bank in the United States, entitled "A Plan for a Modified Central Bank," in which he outlined his plan to avert a panic in the market, and in a speech to the New York Chamber of Commerce he warned, just a few years before the Great Depression, that:

> [U]nless we have a central bank with adequate control of credit resources, this country is going to undergo the most severe and far reaching money panic in its history.

Major known ownership of the Federal Reserve, as of 1983, include: Citibank, Chase, Morgan Guaranty, Manufacturers Hanover, Chemical Bank, Bankers Trust, Bank of New York, J. Henry Schroder Bank, National Bank of North America, and European American Bank, all of which are capitalized by the European banking syndicate. The major shareholders of these banks are related by blood, marriage, and business interests. It's literally a world banking cartel.

The Great Depression

During the first ten years of the 1900s the number of United States banks had doubled to over 20,000; by 1913 only 29 percent of those banks were National banks and they had over 57 percent of all the deposits of the nation - held outside the Cartel. In the first ten years of the new century over 70 percent of corporate funding come from profits rather than loans, and the nation prospered greatly. Unfortunately financial and equity markets were unregulated and prices spiraled out of control leading to inflation. Moreover investment firms started offering margin accounts to purchase stock; essentially brokerage firms were extending credit to investors to make speculative investments. This caused a flurry of inflated stock prices and bad investments. Moreover, by beginning to use a fractional reserve system like the European banks, American banks began to lend over ten times the amount they had on deposit as reserve (some say a low as 1 percent).

The 1907 Banker's Panic occurred when J.P. Morgan, Rockefeller, and other members of the Cartel, as a single unit, pulled their money out of the market and put it into gold and other hard assets (according to their own autobiographies); in other words they dumped their stock. Once the biggest players in banking and industry pulled their money out of the market, other institutional investors started pulling out too, causing a equity death spiral and liquidity crisis, and the average American took the hit. Farms, businesses, and homes went bankrupt and were later purchased for pennies on the dollar by the cartel; the leading banks bought up all their competition and took control of the industry. According to *Life* magazine:

> The Morgan interests took advantage to precipitate the panic (of 1907) guiding it shrewdly as it progresses.

Later in October 1907, in an attempt was made to corner the market on stock of the United Copper Company, and control the copper industry. A group of investors all shorted (dumped) their stock at the same time, causing the market to crash with the hopes of buying it back up at a substantially discounted price, and this led to the downfall of New York City's third-largest trust, the Knickerbocker Trust Company, the competition. This debacle created an even greater loss of confidence in the market. Moreover, all the banks started calling in their loans and would not make new ones which restricted the money supply to the point where business started grinding to a halt, and the Great Depression was set into motion.

In January of 1906, in the heat of this panic created by the Cartel, J.P. Morgan offered to help America by pumping $200 million dollars into the economy, which the government gladly accepted. To do this Morgan simply made up money and distributed to his branches and other banks that he was partners with, and was able to receive interest on it all. At the same time interest rates were raised to tighten the money supply even more, and squeeze the economy even more, so only a small group of bankers had any money and any real power.

In order to gain support for the central bank, members of the banking commission established a $5 million dollar fund to tour the country and "educate" leading businessmen, congressmen, and economic professors about the merits of a central bank, and to lobby the Congress, of course! One economics professor from Princeton named Woodrow Wilson took a keen interest. Wilson had been mentored on the workings of a central bank by one of J.P. Morgan's partners, Bernard Baruch, who was also a Jewish banker and partner in A.A. Houseman & Co. (which was later acquired by Merrill Lynch). According to James Perloff, a prominent historian reporting the incident:

> Baruch brought Wilson to the Democratic Party Headquarters in New York in 1912 leading him like one would lead a poodle on a string. Wilson received an indoctrination course from the leaders convened there.

Woodrow Wilson then stated his policy for solving America's, and the world's, economic crisis. He states:

> All this trouble could be averted if we appointed a committee of six or seven public-spirited men like J.P. Morgan to handle the affairs of our country.

However, there was still great opposition from the Congress and the American people to create a central bank, one of the leading opponents was Charles Lindbergh, Sr., member of congress and father to the famous pilot Charles Lindbergh, Jr., who was first to fly across the Atlantic, who stated his observation at the time, according to Congressman Lindbergh:

Those not favorable to the money trust could be squeezed out of business and the people frightened into demanding changes in the banking and currency laws which the money trust would frame.

The National Monetary Commission was a study group created by the Aldrich Vreeland Act of 1908, led by Senator Nelson Aldrich. The Commission issued thirty reports from 1909 to 1912 that provided information on International banking based on the European model, which formed the basis of the **Federal Reserve Act of 1913**, creating the modern Federal Reserve System.

The plan called for the creation of a National Reserve Association with fifteen regional district branches and forty-six geographically dispersed directors primarily from the banking profession. The Reserve Association would make emergency loans to member banks, create money, and act as the fiscal agent for the U.S. government. State and national banks would have the option of subscribing stock in their local association branch. This was the plan that had been developed at that secret meeting on Jekyll Island in November 1910. At this meeting the key players behind the establishment of the Federal Reserve were present: Senator Nelson Aldrich, Assistant Secretary of the Treasury A. Piatt Andrew, Paul Warburg, Frank Vanderlip, who represented the Rockefeller interests, and other members of the cartel.

Forbes magazine founder Bertie Charles Forbes wrote about the meeting several years later:

Picture a party of the nation's greatest bankers stealing out of New York on a private railroad car under cover of darkness, stealthily riding hundreds of miles South, embarking on a mysterious launch, sneaking onto an island deserted by all but a few servants, living there a full week under such rigid secrecy that the names of not one of them was once mentioned, lest the servants learn the identity and disclose to the world this strangest, most secret expedition in the history of American finance. I am not romancing; I am giving to the world, for the first time, the real story of how the famous Aldrich currency report, the foundation of our new currency system, was written...The utmost secrecy was enjoined upon all. The public must not glean a hint of what was to be done. Senator Aldrich notified each one to go quietly into a private car of which the railroad had received orders to draw up on an unfrequented platform. Off the party set. New York's ubiquitous reporters had been foiled...Nelson (Aldrich) had confided to Henry, Frank, Paul and Piatt that he was to keep them locked up at Jekyll Island, out of the rest of the world, until they had evolved and compiled a scientific currency system for the United States, the real birth of the present Federal Reserve System, the plan done on Jekyll Island in the conference with Paul, Frank and Henry...Warburg is the link that binds the Aldrich system and the present system together. He more than any one man has made the system possible as a working reality.

Frank Vanderlip, the president of Rockefeller's National City Bank, who attended the Jekyl Island meeting, said in the *Saturday Evening Post*:

It was as secretive—indeed as furtive—as any conspirator...discovery we know, simply must not happen, or else all our time and effort would be wasted. If it were to be exposed that our particular group had got together and written a banking bill, that bill would have no chance whatsoever of passage in Congress.

Since the Aldrich Plan essentially gave full control of this monetary system to private bankers, there was strong opposition to it, for fear it would give the money trust too much power over the government. From 1912 to 1913 a subcommittee of the House Committee on Banking and Currency called the **Pujo Committee**, led by Congressman Arsene Pujo, held investigative hearings on the alleged money trust and its interlocking directorates. The congress was very much leaning against the plan. As the Republican Party was being associated with the Aldrich Plan and the money trust, the cartel put its financial and media support behind Democrat Woodrow Wilson who won the election of 1912. Publically Wilson did not support the bank, but privately he did; it was the condition upon which he got Morgan and Rockefeller's support. The banking lobby supports both Republican and Democratic parties; it owns them. The Congress was even threatened with the imposition of Marshall Law if it didn't pass the bill. Representative Charles Lindbergh, Sr. protested:

> The Aldrich Plan is the Wall Street Plan. It means another panic, if necessary, to intimidate the people. Aldrich, paid by the government to represent the people, proposes a plan for the trusts instead.

The Democratic Party had won control of the White House, with Woodrow Wilson, and both chambers of Congress on a party platform clearly stating strong opposition to the "so called Aldrich bill for the establishment of a central bank" and even assured the voters that they would protect the public from "domination by what is known as the money trust." But Wilson was true to his sponsors and advocated the **Currency bill** (H.R. 7837) or the **Glass-Own** bill, which Warburg assured his supporters was essentially the same as the Aldrich Bill that had been defeated before. The primary difference being that instead of the proposed currency being an obligation of the private banks, the new Federal Reserve note was to be an obligation of the U.S. Treasury and membership by the national banks was mandatory, not optional, and that it was brought in through the Democratic Party rather than Republican. After hearings, debates, votes and amendments the proposed legislation was enacted as the **Federal Reserve Act in 1913**.

Upon the passing of the Federal Reserve Act Congressman Lindbergh stated:

> This Act establishes the most gigantic trust on Earth. When the President signs this bill, the invisible government by the Monetary Power will be legalized, the people may not know it immediately but the day of reckoning is only a few years removed...The worst legislative crime of the ages is perpetrated by this banking bill.

New York City mayor John F. Hylan in 1922 stated:

> The real menace of our republic is this invisible government which like a giant octopus sprawls its slimy length over city, state, and nation. Like the octopus of real life, it operates under cover of the self created screen...At the head of this octopus are the Rockefeller Standard Oil interests and a small group of powerful banking houses generally referred to as international bankers. The little coterie of powerful international bankers virtually run the United States government for their own selfish purposes. They practically control both political parties.

Representative Louis Mc Fadden, who was chairman of the House Banking and Currency Commission, publically stated:

> When Woodrow Wilson was nominated...The men who ruled the Democratic Party promised the people if they returned to power there would be no central bank established here while they held the reigns' of government. Thirteen months later that promise was broken and the Wilson administration, under the tutelage of those sinister Wall Street figures who stood behind Colonel House, established here in our free country the worm-eaten monarchial institution of the 'Kings Bank' to control us

from the top downward, and to shackle us from the cradle to the grave.

The Federal Reserve Act

The Federal Reserve Act calls for the creation of both public and private entities. There were to be eight to twelve private regional Federal Reserve Banks (we have twelve), each with its own board of directors and set geographical boundaries. The whole system was headed by a seven-member Federal Reserve Board made up of public officials appointed by the president and confirmed by the Senate from a list drawn from the Federal Reserve itself. In 1935 the board was renamed the Board of Governors of the Federal Reserve System, and they dropped the U.S. secretary of the treasury and comptroller of the currency from the Board (Section 10), so it was completely private. They also created a twelve-member Federal Advisory Committee (Section 12), and a new currency (Section 16), the Federal Reserve Note. In the 1930s the Federal Reserve Act was amended to create the **Federal Open Market Committee** (FOMC), which now has even greater powers to direct all open-market operations of the Federal Reserve member banks.

The Federal Reserve has stock that is privately owned by the member banks; the member banks are publically traded but primary ownership of each is shared by a few common interests. The Federal Reserve does not show its accounts or disclose its activities to the public or even the government, unless it serves them to do so. However, from what has been reported we know the largest founding owners of the Federal Reserve include: Rockefeller's City National Bank, Morgan's National City Bank, and the National Bank of Commerce, which is, in turn, owned by Morgan's Equitable Life, Mutual Life, J.P. Morgan & Co., J.P. Morgan Jr., and Morgan's partners H.P. Davison, Paul Warburg, and Jacobe Schiff, and all of these companies received capitalization from the Rothschild syndicate in Europe. In *The Robber Barons*, Matthew Josephson reports:

> In this campaign of secret alliances he (Morgan) acquired direct control of the National Bank of Commerce; then a part ownership in the First National Bank, allying himself to the very strong and conservative financier, George F. Baker, who headed it; then by means of stock ownership and interlocking directorates he linked to the first named banks of other leading banks, the Hanover, the Liberty, and Chase.

In 1909 Senator Aldrich also introduced a constitutional amendment to establish an **income tax** (that was never formally ratified) to ensure that government debt to the bank would be paid. American's didn't have to pay a federal income tax until the Federal Reserve was created; they are part of the same system. The public was told this system would keep the economy stable, but it was a banking coup, and it has not stabilized our economy. Upon passage of the act, Senator Aldrich stated:

> Before passage of the Act, the New York Bankers could only dominate the reserves of New York. Now, we are able to dominate the bank reserves of the entire country.

Fed 101

How money is made in this new Royal System brought over from Europe:

1) The Federal Reserve Open Market Committee approves the purchase of U.S. bonds (debt instruments) on the open market. In other words, the Fed agrees to give the government the money it wants or to anyone the Fed wants.

2) Those bonds are purchased on the open market; this creates government debt, and the taxpayer is obliged to pay the interest.

3) The Fed pays for the bonds with electronic credits sent to the seller's bank or Treasury. This is money that did not exist before, backed by the security of the U.S. government paying the interest on those bonds from the taxes it collects from the public.

4) Those bonds, or debt instruments (IOUs of the government) serve as an asset on the bank's books. Banks keep reserves on deposit and lend a portion of the balance: they have certain reserve requirements, and they can't lend out all the money they have on deposit (they have to keep some on hand so to speak).

Fractional Reserve Lending is when one bank makes a loan to another entity, based on a percentage of the reserves the bank has on hand; and it typically starts when the Federal Reserve lends money to its member banks. Whoever is in receipt of that money deposits it in some other bank, making it an asset of the bank that just received it as a deposit, and, thus, adding more funds to that bank's cash reserves. A portion of that new deposit can be lent out again, essentially multiplying that money. Whoever the recipient is of that new loan the bank made, he will in turn deposit that money in yet another bank account, now adding to that other bank's reserves. And so it goes creating the money multiplier effect. The more bonds the Fed buys, the more money goes into the street as loans. If the Fed sells bonds and lowers its reserves, it then stops making loans and pulls money out of the economy and shrinks it; like applying a brake, the money slows down.

So, $1 million in bonds gets turned into $10 million in bank account deposits (roughly). To reduce the amount of money in the economy the process is reversed. The Fed sells bonds on the open market to the public, mostly institutional buyers, and the money flows back out of the economy. Loans must also be reduced because reserves are depleted. So a sale of $1 million of bonds removes (roughly) $10 million from the economy, but the Fed makes a fortune each way. The Fed creates a ripple effect in the economy every time it buys or sells bonds on the open market, or raises and lowers its interest rate to other banks.

Congressman Lindbergh explained it this way:

> To cause high prices, all the Federal Reserve Board will do will be to lower the rediscount rate... producing an expansion of credit and a rising stock market; then when...business men are adjusted to these conditions, it can check...prosperity in mid career by arbitrarily raising the rate of interest. It can cause the pendulum of a rising and falling market to swing gently back and forth by slight changes in the discount rate, or cause violent fluctuations by a greater rate variation and in either case it will possess inside information as to financial conditions and advance knowledge of the coming change, either up or down. This is the strangest, most dangerous advantage ever placed in the hands of a special privilege class by any Government that ever existed. The system is private, conducted for the sole purpose of obtaining the greatest possible profits from the use of other people's money. They know in advance when to create panics to their advantage. They also know when to stop panic. Inflation and deflation work equally well for them when they control finance.

The Fed can also expand or diminish market forces and purchasing power by lowering or increasing the interest rates. High interest rates reduce the amount of bank loans for business to grow their business, home loans, car loans, and every other kind of debt financing. Whether you have a job or not, how much you get paid and for how long you work, your entire quality of life that you live depends on the Federal Reserve and what decisions they make. The policies of the Federal Reserve affect citizens personally more than most of the decisions made in Congress, yet they operate without any true government oversight or supervision. The Fed advises the government, not the other way around.

Alan Greenspan, former chairman of the Federal Reserve, summed it up on television, when he said:

> No other agency of government can over ride the actions that we take.

The Great Depression

The United States, and the world, formally plunged into a depression on Black Tuesday, October 29, 1929, when the United States stock market crashed. The tightening of the money supply caused massive layoffs and unemployment, bankruptcies, and loss of homes, farms, and businesses, but it make incredible fortunes for the cartel. Those that control the Fed have insider information that led them to move their assets out of the stock market before it came down in full force, that move out of the market precipitated the crash like a house of cards falling, just like the American Bankers Association threatened just a few years before, and similar to what has happened again to us today.

From 1929-1932 industrial production declined 46 percent, wholesale prices went down 32 percent, foreign trade went down 70 percent, and unemployment, 607 percent. According to Representative Louis T. Mc Fadden, chairman of the House Banking and Currency Committee, speaking on the causes of the Great Depression:

> It was not accidental...It was a carefully contrived occurrence...The International bankers sought to bring about a condition of despair here so that they might emerge as rulers of us all.

Milton Freedman a Nobel Prize-winning economist at the University of Chicago and a leading conservative monetarist and proponent of monetarist policy stated:

> The Federal Reserve definitely caused the Great depression by contracting the amount of currency in circulation by one-third from 1929-1933.

In a dinner honoring Professor Friedman's ninetieth birthday, Federal Reserve Chairman Bernanke addressed professor Friedman and his statement on the depression saying:

> You're right—we did it. We're very sorry. But thanks to you, we won't do it again.

Upon seeing the disaster that had occurred through the formation of the Federal Reserve, President Woodrow Wilson, who helped to create it, lamented (September 25, 1919):

> I am the most unhappy man. I have unwittingly ruined my country. A great individual nation is now controlled by a system of credit. We are no longer governed by free opinion, no longer a government by conviction and the vote of the majority, but a government by the opinion and duress of a small group of dominant men.

Professor Carroll Quigley, professor of history at the Foreign Service School at Georgetown University, and formerly at Princeton and Harvard, speaking on the creation of the Federal Reserve, said:

> Nothing less than to create a world system of financial control in private hands...to dominate the political

system of each country and economy of the world as a whole.

But the very man who brought it about regretted it the most at the end of his life. President Woodrow Wilson said:

> [Our]Great Industrial Nation is controlled by its system of credit. Our system of credit is privately concentrated. The growth of our nation, therefore, and all our activities are in the hands of a few men...who necessarily, by the very reason of their own limitations, chill and check and destroy genuine economic freedom.

> We have come to be one of the most ruled, one of the most completely controlled and dominated governments in the civilized world.

Before he died Wilson said: "I have unwittingly ruined my government."

World War I

The American people were very opposed to getting involved with the First World War. The cartel pressed, but against a strong tide of antiwar sentiment and isolationism throughout the heartland of America, and Wilson was with the progressive party that was against the war. Of course England wanted America's help and part of America wanted to help, but most didn't. But the banking cartel was behind war, after all the money behind the Federal Reserve is European money. So the banks lobbied hard. Warburg was in contact with Britain's secretary of war, and even discussed ways to get the United States into the war, including sacrificing a passenger ship with Americans on it by sending it into German controlled waters. Once the war broke out, Americans ramped up industrial production and incurred more debt doing so.

When World War I was ended, the family feud between royal families in Europe was over, and a group of power emerged from Europe and around the world that was bigger than any country. America came to the stage as a world power and economic player, and the League of Nations ideal led to the United Nations and a view of one global government. Meanwhile, the Federal Reserve and commercial banks also made loans to Germany and Japan, which grew them into prosperous economies again. Using the World Bank and International Monetary Fund (IMF), this same Cartel grew throughout the world and became lenders to other countries. This cartel, through the Federal Reserve, even makes loans to Russia without Americans knowing.

Winston Churchill stated to the London Press in 1922:

> From the days of Sparticus, Wieskhopf, Karl Marx, Trotsky, Rosa Luxemberg, and Emma Goldman, this world conspiracy has been steadily growing. This conspiracy played a definite recognizable role in the tragedy of the French Revolution. It has been the mainspring of every subversive movement during the nineteenth century. And now at last this band of extraordinary personalities from the underworld of the great cities of Europe and America have gripped the Russian people by the hair of their head and have become the undisputed masters of that enormous empire.

In a statement by Congressional Representative Louis T. Mc Fadden:

> The course of Russian History has, indeed, been greatly affected by the operations of international bankers... the Soviet Government has been given United States Treasury funds by the Federal Reserve Board acting through the Chase Bank. England has drawn money from us through the Federal Reserve Banks and re-lent

it at high rates of interest to the Soviet Government. The Dniepersory Dam was built with funds unlawfully taken from the United States Treasury by the corrupt and dishonest Federal Reserve Board and Federal Reserve Banks.

Throughout the history of the United States our founding fathers and presidents have warned the public about the powers and dangers of the Federal Reserve, central banking and fractional reserve lending: Thomas Jefferson, Benjamin Franklin, Alexander Hamilton, and James Madison all warned the public and fought against the bank, while George Washington expressed concern. Later Abraham Lincoln, Andrew Jackson, James Garfield, Theodore Roosevelt, Woodrow Wilson, Franklin D. Roosevelt, and John F. Kennedy spoke out against the Fed, and interestingly they each had either been assassinated or an attempt was made on their life. Since John F. Kennedy, all U.S. presidents have been chosen and financed by the banking cartel.

The Federal Reserve lends to whom it wants and when it wants, without having to inform the public or the government. It also routinely works with other central banks that were also started by the same people. If you want to be a bank today dealing internationally, you need to be in the system, it's now throughout the world, even in Russia and China. The cartel helped develop the whole Chinese banking system, which is becoming the largest in the world. These world-banking laws rule over government laws, and now the money cartel ultimately controls all nations.

Propaganda and The New World Order

Through all the years that the international bankers pushed their governments to create central banks in order to control currency, commerce, and trade, their greatest opposition was from the citizens themselves. Most of the time these banking transactions are carried on in secret, and this is what gives them tremendous power; to make decisions without being questioned or to be impeded by competition or public opinion. The less regulated the banking industry is, the more power they have. Before the age of radio, television, or the Internet, public information was reported through newspapers and magazines, which President Theodore Roosevelt already stated were owned and directed by the cartel or money trust as he put it and this is still true today.

During the late 1800s the behavioral science of psychology was developing, and the famous psychoanalyst Dr. Sigmund Freud was revealing how the subconscious mind works and how people are motivated and respond to external forces and information (suggestion). Freud's nephew, Edward Louis Bernays (1891-1995), along with columnists Walter Lippmann and Ivy Lee created the industry of public relations (PR) and developed the commercial use of propaganda, and these men played a leading role in developing scientific techniques of molding public opinion and what they called "the engineering of consent." The opening paragraph of Bernays's book called *Propaganda* reads as follows:

> The conscious and intelligent manipulation of the organized habits and opinions of the masses is an important element in democratic society. Those who manipulate this unseen mechanism of society constitute an invisible government which is the true ruling power of our country.

Bernays goes on further to say:

> We are governed, our minds molded, our tastes formed, our ideas suggested, largely by men we have never heard of...Our invisible governors are, in many cases, unaware of the identify of their fellow members in the inner cabinet...it remains a fact that in almost every act of our daily lives, whether in the sphere of politics or business, in our social conduct or our ethical thinking, we are dominated by the relatively small number of persons—a trifling fraction of our hundred and twenty million—who understand the mental processes and social patterns of the masses.

Some of Benays's public accomplishments were: growing tobacco market share by spinning the acceptability of women smoking, the campaign was called Torches of Freedom during a period that women were fighting for their freedom and rights as citizens. Bernays had models marching in a parade smoking Lucky Strike cigarettes in front of eager photographers, and it worked. Clairol hair products wanted to introduce a hair dye women could use on themselves at home rather than have to go to the salon, and he devised the slogan Only her hair dresser knows for sure. He promoted the idea of adding fluoridation of water for public health, as well as forming many political public opinions for candidates and presidents. But Bernays, Lippmann, and Ivy were put to their best uses in promoting war in the public's mind. Woodrow Wilson hired propagandists to rally the American people to go to war for the European cause. In his 1965 autobiography, Bernays (a Jew keep in mind) recalls a dinner at his home in 1933, about which he recounts:

> Karl von Weigand, foreign correspondent of the Hearst newspapers, an old hand at interpreting Europe and just returned from Germany, was telling us about Goebbels and his propaganda plans to consolidate Nazi power. Goebbels had shown Weigand his propaganda library, the best Weigand had ever seen. Goebbels, said Weigand, was using my book *Crystallizing Public Opinion* as a basis for his destructive campaign against the Jews of Germany. This shocked me...Obviously the attack on the Jews of Germany was no emotional outburst of the Nazis, but a deliberate, planned campaign (to mold public opinion in Germany against the Jews).

Pulitzer Prize-winning columnist Walter Lippman, one of the founding editors of *The New Republic*, was instrumental in shifting the American public's views for the First and Second World Wars. Lippmann became an adviser to President Woodrow Wilson and helped him draft his Fourteen Points speech, which laid the foundation of the United Nations and the **New World Order** of a global government. Ivy Lee, the third founder of public relations, primarily worked for the Rockefellers and became an inaugural member of the Council on Foreign Relations, a think tank founded by the cartel in 1921. American author Upton Sinclair dubbed him "Poison Ivy" after Lee tried to send bulletins saying that the coal miners who were striking in Colorado died of an overturned stove, when in fact they were shot by the Colorado militia in the Ludlow Massacre.

PR provides damage control and molds public opinion by how the information is presented in the media; information is typically put in a context before being presented to the viewers, so their mind is already leaning a certain direction when new information is presented (context), or the repetition of the same opinion over and over develops that idea in the viewer or listener's mind at a subconscious level. If it can be perceived that a group consensus has been made by or through the media, then more people are likely to go along with it. This is called manufactured consent or engineered consent; the perception is that everyone is saying it, so it must be true. The United States media is the best in the world at manufacturing consent.

One of the most powerful ways to manipulate people is to put them in fear, constant fear, so fear is used again and again to motivate people to do what a government or a corporation wants like a herding instinct, people are conditioned to follow. Consent is managed through the news media and public opinion is created before being presented to viewers and listeners. Once most people have heard it enough times their mind automatically develops that perception being given; we are hypnotized by the television and radio and thoughts are created for you to think, and most people will think them. We think what we are told and don't realize the thoughts we have were formed by others that we accepted in a suggestible state. Managing public opinion is a multibillion-dollar industry, and it's down to a science.

Woodrow Wilson had another adviser who played a key role in foreign policy named Edward M. House or Colonel House (1858-1938); he was such a close adviser that he actually lived at the White House. House was a banker, who helped create the League of Nations, the World Court, and laid the groundwork for establishing the Council on Foreign Relations (CFR), along with David Rockefeller and J.P. Morgan. House represented the cartel, which was anxious to enter the war, as wars create massive debt, which makes massive profits for them from the interest on the loans. It's the proven means to create deficit spending, from which the cartel profits.

Entering World War II took the United States out of the depression, and into a period of economic boom and prosperity; the United States became a superpower. The postwar years were a period of economic boom for Western economies after World War II and lasted into the 1970s. The Golden Age of capitalism drove the powerful war machine built up fighting the Germans and Japanese, and now retooled itself for a new era of consumerism. This boom ended with the collapse of the Bretton Woods system in 1971, and then the oil crisis of 1973, and the stock market crash of 1973 and 1974, which ultimately created the recession of the later 1970s.

Bretton Woods, the IMF, and OPEC

The Bretton Woods system of monetary policy established financial and commercial relationships among the world's global powers. In July of 1944, just after World War II, 730 delegates from all forty-four Allied nations met at Mount Washington Hotel in Bretton Woods, New Hampshire, for the United Nations Monetary and Financial Conference. During the first three weeks of July of that year, members of the same banking cartel established the International Monetary Fund (IMF) and the International Bank for Reconstruction and Development (IBRD), which evolved into what we call the World Bank. The agreement was for each nation to fix and maintain the exchange rate of its currency, plus or minus 1 percent, and peg their currency to the price of gold as a universal standard of value.

The IMF was supposed to be able to provide a bridge financing for any temporary imbalances of payments, which were

inevitable, and profitable. This helped stabilize world currencies and fostered world trade, but in 1971 President Nixon was
being heavily influenced by Secretary of State Henry Kissinger,
a former employee of the Rockefellers and key member of
the Council on Foreign Relations who wrote America's foreign
policy while serving on the National Security Council. Kissinger
was encouraging a military buildup during the Vietnam War
and wanted to open up the money supply through debt financing and taking us off the gold standard, which is what brought
us into massive debt that led to the recession of that era.

In 1973 oil-producing nations came together to try to gain
more control over oil pricing and formed the Organization of
Arab Petroleum Exporting Countries (**OPEC)**, and they pro-
claimed an oil embargo in response to resupplying Israel's military during the Yom Kippur war. This caused a radical spike in
oil prices, and a lack of fuel at the pumps around the world,
which exacerbated the recession by causing greater inflation.
Higher oil prices lead to higher transportation costs, which
affects all manufactured goods, agriculture, energy, heating,
price of plastics, and fertilizers, which use petroleum as their
base. By 1974 the price of oil had quadrupled to nearly $12
per barrel. However, people and companies were able to con-
serve energy and political and financial pressures eventually
brought stability to the oil market again.

In 1961 The Organization for Economic Cooperation and
Development (OECD) brought thirty-four counties together
to provide a platform to compare policy experiences and find
solutions to common problems facing each economy. According
to their records real Gross Domestic Product (GDP) grew an
impressive rate of over 4 percent each year during the 1950s,
and nearly 5 percent a year during the 1960s, but dropped to
only 3 percent in the 1970s and 2 percent in the 1980s, so
clearly our current monetarist monetary system was not doing
very well. Other metrics include an average global annual inflation of 3.9 percent and average unemployment in the United

States of 4.8 percent, both of which are more than twice what is healthy. According to Martin Wolf, associate editor of the *London Financial Times*, we saw only thirty-eight financial crises during in the twenty-seven years before the Crises, and 139 in the twenty-four years after (1973-97). During this time we also saw a rapid increase in the amount of imports that led to a giant trade imbalance; in other words, we were governed very poorly using a monetarist system.

Keynesian versus Monetarist

There are two primary camps of economic theory used in our world economy: Keynesian and monetarist. John Maynard Keynes (1883-1946) maintained a demand-side perspective, where industry, government, and the money supply should maintain a consistent growth rate and not exceed demand, whereas, supply-side or monetarist theory allows for less restraint and was developed at the University of Chicago. It is also important to note that the Rockefellers, who founded the Federal Reserve, also founded and funded the University of Chicago and are the one of the biggest supporters of the schools of business and economics. Keynes put the government in charge, but the Chicago School puts the banks in charge. Keynes also focused monetary policy toward creating jobs and lowering unemployment, whereas the monetarist approach believes the market should dictate employment and pricing, which means the Fed will dictate the economic expansion or contraction. In either school, maintaining the money supply and credit availability was the key.

Monetarism also recommends restraint of fiscal spending by the government, but that condition is rarely met even by those professing it as the best model. In fact, most governments use a little of both models, but we really all just do whatever the Fed thinks. Monetarist policies advocate what has been referred to as a trickle-down affect, as businesses prosper they will hire more people and contribute more taxes from revenues, and grow the economy; unfortunately each year the federal government deficit spends, typically for a war or some new terror, and the average American has suffered from higher taxes, inflation, unemployment, and a weakened economy as a result.

Our buying power continues to diminish, our prosperity and net worth continue to decline, while our debt keeps growing; most people live under a tremendous stress of debt. One of the glaring weaknesses of monetarist policy in retrospect is the widening gap between the very wealthy and the middle class, as well as an increase in criminal actions amongst our titans of banking, business, and government when unregulated. We are developing a criminal consciousness at the highest levels of government and banking; cheating, deceiving, and even lying become acceptable for the sake of winning. The corporate consciousness that exists today is not one that is in the best interest of the whole, but what makes the most money for the select few on the top, the 1 percent. The money has literally moved from the prospering middle class to the ultra rich. CEOs make hundreds of millions of dollars and the cartel is at the top of this pyramid. We are all becoming enslaved through debt—individuals, corporations, cities, counties, states, and national governments are all debt encumbered and beholding to banks.

In a letter by President Franklin Delano Roosevelt, America's thirty-second president, who served from just before through most of World War II, we gain insight into world power. He came from a prominent New York banking family, and led the building of our "Arsenal of Democracy," which enabled the Allies to win the second world war. His uncle, Fredrick was one of the original members of the Federal Reserve Board. Roosevelt spoke very openly about world power:

> The real truth of the matter is, as you and I know, that a financial element in the large centers has owned the government ever since the days of Andrew Jackson.

When Roosevelt was inaugurated in 1933, the United States was in the depths of the depression and over two million people were homeless; thirty-two states had closed their banks and the New York Federal Reserve Bank was unable to open because of huge sums being withdrawn in previous days. Beginning with his inaugural address Roosevelt began blaming the economic crisis on the bankers who he said were taking advantage of the people to make a profit:

> Practices of the unscrupulous moneychangers stand indicted in the court of public opinion, rejected by the hearts and minds of men. True they have tried, but their efforts have been cast in the pattern of an outworn tradition. Faced by failure of credit they have proposed only the lending of money. Stripped of the lure of profit by which to induce our people to follow their false leadership, they have resorted to exhortations, pleading tearfully for restored confidence...The moneychangers have fled from their high seats in the temple of civilization. We may now restore that temple to the ancient truths. The measure of the restoration lies in the extent to which we apply social values more noble than mere monetary profit.

Germany

One of the most shocking stories about the Federal Reserve discovered within the annals of United States History is the role America played in helping Adolph Hitler rise to power. Only eight years before Adolph Hitler would invade Poland, United States Representative Louis McFadden, chairman of the House

Banking and Currency Committee, warned the Congress that Americans were paying for Hitler's rise to power, stating:

> After World War I, Germany fell into the hands of the German international bankers. Those bankers bought her and they now own her, lock, stock, and barrel. They have purchased her industries, they have mortgages on her soil, they control her production, they control all her public utilities...Through the Federal Reserve Board...over $30 billions of American money...has been pumped into Germany. You have all heard of the money that is being spent in Germany...modernistic dwellings, her great planetariums, her gymnasiums, her swimming pools, her fine public highways, her perfect factories. All this was done on our money. All this was given to Germany through the Federal Reserve Board.
>
> The Federal Reserve Board...has pumped so many billions of dollars into Germany that they dare not name the total.

President Roosevelt's words in 1936 summarize the condition we face today:

> These economic "royalists" complain that we seek to overthrow the institutions of America. What they really complain of is that we seek to take away their power. Against economic tyranny such as this, the American citizen could only appeal to the organize power of government. The collapse of 1929 showed despotism for what it was. The election of 1932 was the people's mandate to end it, and under that mandate it is being ended.

As history shows, Roosevelt was never able to end the Federal Reserve, however, Americans did experience a better standard of living as a result of the boost in spending in the economy; but that better living they got eventually created an gigantic deficit that weighted down the economy for future generations, just as the Reagan arms race with the Soviet Union placed a heavy burden on the American economy and taxpayers for future generations. The campaign promises were for reduced government spending, but the stated objectives were to increase defense spending to record deficits. Social programs were cut, but overall spending increased dramatically, and this debt has placed a heavy burden on the American taxpayers.

The Military Industrial Complex

At the end of World War II the United States had half the world's manufacturing capacity, and one-third of its gold stocks. We produced twice as much oil as the rest of the world combined, and Americans made about twice as much money as they did before the war. The United States became a superpower. During World War II a massive industry was developed to support the military, and it yielded much power in Washington and has ever since. Just look at the revolving door between key executives in government like the Department of Defense and the military who leave and return between the government and private-sector military contractors; the private wealth that is made from this inside circle is criminal, and the public is robbed. Historically, the banks are always politically for war because it's both patriotic to support a noble cause in case of attack, but all too often it is also self-serving as history teaches us. In a farewell address to the American people, one of America's greatest generals and thirty-fourth president of the United States, Dwight D. Eisenhower, clearly warned American citizens (January 17, 1961):

> A vital element in keeping the peace is our military establishment. Our arms must be mighty, ready for instant action, so that no potential aggressor may be tempted to risk his own destruction...

This conjunction of an immense military establishment and a large arms industry is new in the American experience. The total influence—economic, political, [and] even spiritual—is felt in every city, every statehouse, every office of the federal government. We recognize the imperative need for this development. Yet we must not fail to comprehend its grave implications. Our toil, resources, and livelihood are all involved; so is the very structure of our society. In the councils of government, **we must guard against the acquisition of unwarranted influence, whether sought or unsought, by the military-industrial complex**. The potential for the disastrous rise of misplaced power exists and will persist. We must never let the weight of this combination endanger our liberties or democratic processes. We should take nothing for granted. Only an alert and knowledgeable citizenry can compel the proper meshing of the huge industrial and military machinery of defense with our peaceful methods and goals so that security and liberty may prosper together.

The Stockholm International Peace Research Institute (SIPRI) is an independent international institute dedicated to research into conflict, armaments, arms control, and disarmament that was established in 1966. SIRPI reports total world spending on military expenses in 2009 was $1.531 trillion dollars, and approximately half was spent by the United States alone. Most of our representatives, in both parties, receive massive support through lobbyists in Washington, and as part of the same cartel as banking and oil, they jointly share a manufactured consent of world domination of natural resources as being in America's national self-interest, to defend in war. Thus, we have grown into a war economy, which means we need wars or terror to keep our military contractors busy or find a better application of their resources in America.

The cartel drives the policy; they do this through the United Nations, the Council on Foreign Relations, financial relationships with leading universities (Harvard, Princeton, Yale, University of Chicago, etc.), media, charities, think tanks, lobbying, as well as the Central Intelligence Agency, and now Homeland Security. The people who created, fund, and run these organizations are all the same people; these are the people who run our government, and to a large extent the entire world economy. The world is run through a series of structures to compartmentalize and distribute the power.

The United Nations

The United Nations was founded in 1945 after the Second World War to replace the League of Nations, which was attempted after the first world war; its stated aims are: facilitating cooperation in international law, international security, economic development, social progress, human rights, and achievement of world peace. It has a General Assembly, a Security Council, the Economic and Social Council and an International Court of Justice. Within its association are the World Health Organization (WHO), the World Food Program (WFP), and the United Nations Children's Fund (UNICEF). Nelson Rockefeller generously arranged financing, after an initial offer to locate it on the Rockefeller family estate. The $8.5 million needed was funded by Nelson's grandfather John D. Rockefeller, Jr., who donated it to the city and was keen on its development as part of his stated intent to build a global government.

The Council on Foreign Relations

Founded in 1921 in New York, the Council on Foreign Relations (CFR) is considered to be the nation's most influential foreign-policy think tank; it also publishes *Foreign Affairs*, which is considered the leading journals on foreign affairs. The CFR also has a sister organization in Great Britain called the Royal Institute for International Affairs or Chatham House. The stated mission of the Council is as:

> [A] resource for its members, government officials, business executives, journalists, educators and students, civic and religious leaders, and other interested citizens in order to help them better understand the world and the foreign policy choices facing the United States and other countries.

The Council of Foreign Relations (CFR) was founded by Edward M. House, Walter Lippmann, Paul Warburg, John D. Rockefeller, J.P. Morgan, John Dulles and their circle, and the current headquarters was donated by Harold Irving Pratt, who served as director of the Standard Oil Company and as well as Director of the CFR from 1923-1939. Its think tank, the David Rockefeller Studies Program, is composed of about fifty adjunct and full-time scholars from the best universities and government, who make recommendations to the presidential administrations, regardless of party. Today, there are over 5,000 members, including the most influential people in Washington. Members include more than a dozen American Secretaries of State, former national security advisors, bankers, lawyers, former CIA members, publishers, and senior members of the media.

The most important people in government, education, industry, banking and the military are members of the Council, the most influential people running our country receive advise from this group; there is manufactured consent within it for a New World Order and global government, and these some 5,000 members are the ones at the top of world government, banking and trade.

Detractors of the CFR had their concerns expressed in an article published in Harpers in 1958:

> The most powerful clique in these (CFR) groups has one objective in common: they want to bring about the surrender of the sovereignty and the national independence of the U.S. They want to end national boundaries and racial and ethnic loyalties supposedly to increase business and ensure world peace. What they strive for would inevitably lead to dictatorship and loss of freedoms by the people. The CFR was founded for the purpose of promoting disarmament and submergence of U.S. sovereignty and national independence into an all-powerful one-world government.

David Rockefeller was chairman of the board from 1970 to 1985, and Dick Cheney also served as chairman. Presidents George Bush, Sr. and Jimmy Carter were both very involved, and its greatest proponents for a New World Order and one world government; Henry Kissinger plays a central role and developed much of this thinking there and applied it to the National Security Council (NSC) and to America's national foreign policy. Testifying before the United States Senate committee on foreign relations in 1950, Warburg, representing CFR, stated in testimony before the United States Senate:

> We shall have world government whether or not we like it. The only question is whether world government will be achieved by conquest or consent.

Speaking before the Council on Foreign Relations in June 1991, David Rockefeller said:

> We are grateful to the *Washington Post*, the *New York Times*, *Time* magazine and all the other great publications whose directors have attended our meetings and respected their promises of discretion for almost forty years. It would have been impossible for us to develop

our plan for the world if we had been subjected to the light of publicity during those years. But now the world is more sophisticated and prepared to march towards a world government. The supra national sovereignty of an intellectual elite and world bankers is surely preferable to the national auto-determination practiced in the past centuries.

In 2002 David Rockefeller published his autobiography *Memoirs* and on page 405 he emphatically states, speaking on the Council on Foreign Relations:

Some even believe we are part of a secret cabal working against the best interests of the United States, characterizing my family and me as "internationalists" and of conspiring with others around the world to build a more integrated global political and economic structure—one world, if you will. If that's the charge, I stand guilty, and I am proud of it.

Bilderberg Group and the Trilateral Commission

The Bilderberg Group is an annual unofficial, invitation only, conference of around 130 of the most influential people of the world from politics, banking, business, military, and media. The group was named after the hotel that the first meeting took place in 1954, the Hotel de Bilderberg in the Netherlands. Prince Bernhard of Lippe-Biesterfeld, the father of Queen Beatrix of the Netherlands, was the first chairman of the Steering Committee and other European royalty have followed. Members of the banking cartel and American industry mix and share ideas with royalty and other world leaders and seek answers in private without concern of reporters so they can speak freely. Who shows up and what subjects were discussed is posted on their website for the public to read, and they should, but the press is not allowed to report.

Denis Healey (Baron Healey), former secretary of state for defense and chancellor of the exchequer for Great Britain and Bilderberg founder and head of the steering committee, has said:

> To say we are striving for a one-world government is exaggerated, but not wholly unfair. Those of us in Bilderberg felt we couldn't go on forever fighting one another for nothing and killing people and rendering millions homeless. So we felt that a single community throughout the world would be a good thing.

The Trilateral Commission is a private organization founded and funded in 1973 by David Rockefeller to foster closer cooperation among the United States, Europe, and Japan; it spun off from the Council on Foreign Relations. According to Rockefeller the Trilateral Commission could "be of help to government by providing measured judgment." Former National Security Adviser for President Jimmy Carter and professor at Columbia University Zbigniew Brzezinski helped organize the group, along with Alan Greenspan and Paul Volcker, both now former heads of the Federal Reserve but their training was with Rockefellers Council on Foreign Relations and the Trilateral Commission; this is the university for the cartels most elite, the training ground for presidents, secretaries of state and world bankers. This is where the ideas are formed to implement the New World Order of world government, law, banking, and business, a kind of Fabian socialism, where a certain elite rule. This group becomes the basis for a continuity of government and commerce; in the event of the possible destruction of government those elite could keep the world running and keep running the world. A similar intellectual Darwinism is illustrated in Herman Hesse's classic book the *Glass Bead Game*, where an intellectual elite compete to rule the world.

Today it consists of approximately 300 bankers, corporate CEOs, and leading politicians; President Jimmy Carter attended their first plenary meeting in 1976. Political historian and Massachusetts Institute of Technology professor Norm Chomsky observed in his book *Radical Priorities*:

> Perhaps the most striking feature of the new Administration is the role played in it by the Trilateral Commission. The mass media had little to say about this matter during the presidential campaign—in fact, the connection of the Carter group to the Commission was recently selected as 'the best censored news story of 1976—and it has not received the attention that it might have since the administration took office. All of the top positions in the government—the office of President, Vice-President, Secretary of State, Defense and Treasury—are held by members of the Trilateral Commission, and the National Security Adviser was its director. Many lesser officials also came from this group. It is rare for such an easily identified private group to play such a prominent role in an American Administration.

If you look at the administrations of Richard Nixon, Gerald Ford, Jimmy Carter, Ronald Reagan, George H.W. Bush, Bill Clinton, George W. Bush, and Barak Obama, they all had been affiliated with, studied with, and made their alliances through one or several of these cartel-based, Rockefeller-funded, organizations. Whether Republican or Democrat, they get the same training and financial support; it's an indoctrination into world government that is now a requirement of being selected for high office within either party. The elite have engineered a consent in worldview and created a collective consciousness in attaining it; every one of America's recent presidents has advocated a New World Order.

Look up the key positions of vice president, or secretaries of the major cabinets, such as Secretary of State or Defense, or the National Security Advisor, they all get their training and make their alliances from within this same sphere of influence. Every once in awhile an outsider like Ross Perot or Ralph Nader will stand up to challenge this second tier of government, but the whole system of finance and government is run by these same people. It's not a conspiracy. It's the state of consciousness that rules this world. Everyone in it thinks they are doing something really good, and in some ways they are.

These aspirations within government have also met with much opposition, in his 1964 book *With No Apologies* United States Senator Barry Goldwater stated:

> The Trilateral Commission is intended to be the vehicle for multinational consolidation of the commercial and banking interests by seizing control of the political government of the United States. The Trilateral Commission represents a skillful, coordinated effort to seize control and consolidate the four centers of power political, monetary, intellectual, and ecclesiastical. What the Trilateral Commission intends is to create a worldwide economic power superior to the political governments of the nation states involved. As managers and creators of the system, they will rule the future.

The Cabinet

To gain a perspective on how much influence these cartel institutions have, we have only to observe the backgrounds of the current administration. President Barak Obama worked for Business International Corp. (BI), now the Economist Group, right out of college; it's 50 percent owned by the Rothschild consortium and is internationally believed to be a front for the Central Intelligence Agency (and British intelligence), and most of his financial backing to run for the senate or presidency came from the cartel. He's been groomed for the job of president over many years; the cartel is his financial sponsor, and his entire cabinet is one cartel team.

United States Treasury secretary Timothy Geithner (former) president of the Federal Reserve Bank of New York, started his career working for Henry Kissinger and is also a member of CFR, Trilateral, and Bilderberg. Secretary of State Hillary Clinton and her deputy, also CFR and Bilderberg, and her husband, the former President Bill Clinton, was also on the Trilateral Commission. Ambassador to the United Nations Susan Rice is on the Trilateral Commission. National Security Advisor General James L. Jones a member of CFR, Trilateral and Bilderberg, as is his deputy; Special Envoy Henry Kissinger a key member of CFR, Trilateral, and Bilderberg; Chairman of Economic Recovery Committee Paul Volker, former chairman of the Federal Reserve and member of CFR, Trilateral, and Bilderberg; Director of National Security (intelligence) Admiral Dennis C. Blair also a member of CFR, Trilateral, and Bilderberg; and so are our Secretary of Defense Robert Gates and Deputy Secretary of State James Stevenson, as well as special envoys Richard Hass and Richard Holbrook, and many others. All the main players in the Obama Administration, as well as those in the preceding Bush Administration, have been indoctrinated in one-world government thinking. You don't climb the ladder of national government or world power without this system helping and directing you, regardless of political party.

All these organizations that have been sponsored by the banking cartel serve to gather and disseminate information; what they have in common is a view that serves their common interests of a one world government that they decided is best run by them. These think tanks and nongovernment organizations (NGOs) that advise the government, lobby the congress, and write the bills for representatives to present in congress, are mouthpieces of the same system. The same small group of families show up again and again behind each organization and throughout each structure. John F. Kennedy's father, Joseph Kennedy, stated in the *New York Times* "Fifty men run America, and that's a high figure."

When president John F. Kennedy came into office, he came as an outsider to the banking cartel, the Council on Foreign Relations, and their extensive network. Pulitzer Prize-winning historian and social critic, Arthur M. Schlesinger, writing about President Kennedy first learning about the cartel and what he called the New York establishment:

> In particular, he was little acquainted with the New York financial and legal community that arsenal of talent which had so long furnished a steady supply of always orthodox and often able people to Democratic as well as Republican administrations. This community was the heart of the American Establishment. It's household deities were Henry Stimson and Elihu Root; its present leaders, Robert Lovett and John J. McCloy; its front organizations, the Rockefeller, Ford and Carnegie foundations and the Council on Foreign Relations; its organs, the New York Times and Foreign Affairs.

After getting an orientation in the White House, President Kennedy began to make the reforms he promised the people who elected him, but those changes stood in clear opposition to those who had maintained the power for so long. Kennedy felt thwarted and explained it publically this way:

> We are opposed around the world by a monolithic and ruthless conspiracy, a system that has conscripted vast human and material resources into the building of a tightly knit highly efficient machine, that perceptions are concealed and not published, its mistakes are buried

not headlined, its dissenters' are silenced not praised, no expenditure is questioned, no rumors printed, no secrets revealed.

The New World Order

What is the New World Order? It means different things to different people, and gaining clarity as to what our presidents, national security advisers, international bankers, or royalty think of as the New World Order is something very important for every citizen to think about. The New World Order is a term that has been used deliberately by each United States president, the national security advisers and secretaries of state; it's a term used quite a bit amongst those in the Council on Foreign Relations, the Trilateral Commission, as well as international bankers and the Federal Reserve. Much of this vision appears to be a beautiful thing, but so much also appears to be cloaked in secrecy. So, it's worth looking at its possible meanings and to create a dialog within the population to consider its merits.

The New World Order can refer to any period of history evidencing a dramatic change in world politics and the balance of power between nations; it more often than not includes some vision of a singular world government; some use of the term refers specifically to a conspiracy theory in which a secret elite is conspiring to rule the world by means of world government and globalization. Statesmen like Woodrow Wilson and Winston Churchill began using the term New World Order in the beginning of the twentieth century to refer to a new balance of power after the world wars with an ideal of global governance between nations to solve the world's political, military, and financial problems. These ideals led to the creation of the United Nations, NATO, the Breton Woods monetary system, and the General Agreement on Tariffs and Trade (GATT).

The term was more fully developed in a book by H.G. Wells called *The New World Order*, which was published in 1939. In this context the New World Order is a synonym for the establishment of a scientifically coordinated world state and planned economy—the kind of Fabian socialism in which Wells was involved. In this context the New World Order is more of a totalitarian theocracy led by an intelligentsias or illuminati. In *The New World Order*, H.G. Wells explains the creation of a new world currency:

> Directly we grasp this not very obscure truth that there can be, and are, different sorts of money dependent on the economic usages or system in operation, which are not really interchangeable, then it becomes plain that a collectivist world order, whose fundamental law is such a Declaration of Rights as we have sketched, will have to carry on its main, its primary operations at least with a new world money, a specially contrived money, differing in its nature from any sort of money conventions that have hitherto served human needs. It will be issued against the total purchasable output of the community in return for the workers' services to the community.

Some government representatives see the New World Order as being more Orwellian, a conspiracy or shadow government controlled by the world bankers, royalty, or Jews; there is a very strong antiglobalist movement within both the Republican and Democratic parties even as more globalist rhetoric is being conveyed in almost all the think thanks, policy boards, and media being used today. The best source to learn more about the New World Order, as the term is being used in government today, is to study the work of the Council on Foreign Relations, which is reflected in their periodical *Foreign Affairs,* which is available to the public.

President George H.W. Bush, in his September 11, 1990 speech to a joint session of the U.S. Congress titled "Towards a New World Order," stated his objectives for a post cold war global governance:

> Until now, the world we've known has been a world divided - a world of barbed wire and concrete block, conflict, and cold war. Now we can see a new world coming into view. A world in which there is the very real prospect of a New World Order.

Congressional Representative and second president of the John Birch Society, holds a very negative view of this theory stating:

> The drive of the Rockefellers and their allies is to create a one-world government, combining super-capitalism and Communism under the same tent, all under their control...Do I mean conspiracy? Yes, I do. I am con-vinced there is such a plot, international in scope, gen-erations old in planning, and incredibly evil in intent.

Another valuable perspective of the New World Order can be gained from the U.S. Central Intelligence Agency (CIA) in a February 2000 document from the Chairman of the National Intelligence Council, John C. Gannon, called "The CIA in the New World Order: Intelligence Challenges Through 2015." In summarizing the next fifteen years in this report Gannon states:

> Globalization will provide mankind with the unprec-edented opportunity to improve the quality of human life across the planet; but progress will be hampered by economic volatility, by the political and security impli-cations of sharpening inequalities in income, and by the growing threat from multiple, relatively small-scale programs of weapons of mass destruction.

In what they call "**Global Trends 2015**" the CIA explains the first driver of the world economy is global population trends;

the existing population trend is increasing from approximately 6 billion today to 7.2 billion by 2015, with 95 percent of this growth taking place in developing countries. It also states that growing populations and increased per capita income will drive demand for oil up as much as 60 percent of current levels by 2015 and that they expect world per capita income to increase at an average annual rate of at least 2 percent between now and 2015. They project that world food stocks will be sufficient to meet overall global needs by 2015. The fifth trend in the report is even more telling, and states:

> The relative power and influence of many nation-states will continue to erode over the next fifteen years, while transnational networks of all kinds will almost certainly grow in number, economic power, and political significance.

According to this CIA report:

> Globalization and the permeability of borders to the flow of people, goods, and information are all combining to erode state sovereignty. The state's power is shifting in three directions: outward to nonstate actors, downward to sub national and local levels of government, and upward, to a certain degree, to regional and international institutions and legal regimes.

Writing for the Council on Foreign Relations in *Foreign Affairs*, economist Jagdish N. Bhagwati states that the fear of globalization began historically in the East, not the West. He concludes, in a January 2011 op-ed article titled "Globalization Marches On":

> By contract, the East generally embraced the fearful view that, as the Chilean sociologist Oswaldo Sunkel put it, integration into the international economy would lead to disintegration of the national economy. Many intellectuals shared this dark anti-globalization vision,

and policymakers in much of the East were not far behind.

President George H.W. Bush spoke at great lengths on the New World Order and a globalized government:

> The world can therefore seize the opportunity [Persian Gulf crisis] to fulfill the long-held promise of a New World Order where diverse nations are drawn together in common cause to achieve the universal aspirations of mankind.

> As old threats recede new threats emerge. The quest for the New World Order is in part a challenge to keep the dangers of disorder at bay. We should build on the successes of Desert Storm to give new shape and momentum to this New World Order. Only when this transformation is complete will we be able to take full measure of the opportunities presented by this new and evolving World Order.

> The New World Order is really a tool for addressing the new world of possibilities. This Order gains its mission and shape not just from shared interests, but from shared ideals.

Strobe Talbot, President Clinton's deputy secretary of state, was quoted in *Time* magazine July 1992 as saying:

> In the next century, nations as we know it will be obsolete; all states will recognize a single, global authority. National sovereignty wasn't such a great idea after all.

James Warburg, speaking to the Senate Foreign Relations Committee in 1950:

> We shall have world government whether or not you like it, by conquest or consent.

Richard Gardner, writing for the April 1974 issue of *Foreign Affairs*:

> The New World Order will have to be built from the bottom up rather than from the top down...but in the end run around national sovereignty, eroding it piece by piece will accomplish much more than the old fashioned frontal assault.

H.G. Wells, in his book The New World Order (1939) he states:

> "[W]hen the struggle seems to be drifting definitely towards a world social democracy, there may still be very great delays and disappointments before it becomes an efficient and beneficent world system. Countless people...will hate the new world order...and will die protesting against it. When we attempt to evaluate its promise, we have to bear in mind the distress of a generation or so of malcontents, many of them quite gallant and graceful-looking people.

When former director of the Council on Foreign Relations and secretary of state under president Richard Nixon, Henry Kissinger, addressed the General Assembly of the United Nations in October of 1975, he stated:

> My country's history, Mr. President, tells us that it is possible to fashion unity while cherishing diversity, that common action is possible despite the variety of races, interests, and beliefs we see here in this chamber. Progress and peace and justice are attainable. So we say to all peoples and governments: Let us fashion together a new world order.

At the Bilderberg Conference in Evians, France in 1991, Dr. Henry Kissinger also had this to say:

Today, America would be outraged if U.N. troops entered Los Angeles to restore order [referring to the 1991 LA riot]. Tomorrow they will be grateful! This is especially true if they were told that there was an outside threat from beyond, whether real or promulgated, that threatened our very existence. It is then that all peoples of the world will plead to deliver them from this evil (Terrorists). The one thing every man fears is the unknown. When presented with this scenario, individual rights will be willingly relinquished for the guarantee of their well-being granted to them by the World Government.

President George Bush (January 1991):

If we do not follow the dictates of our inner moral compass and stand up for human life, then his lawlessness will threaten the peace and democracy of the emerging new world order we now see, this long dreamed-of vision we've all worked toward for so long.

Nelson Rockefeller, vice president under Gerald Ford, cartel leader, and globalist visionary, speaking at the Council on Foreign Relations:

Religious leader Pope Paul VI, delegates to international organizations, public officials, gentlemen of the press, teachers and educators. All of you must realize that you have your own part to play in the construction of a New World Order.

Adolph Hitler: "National Socialism will use its own revolution for the establishing of a new world order."

So we can see from the discussion of the New World Order from the perspective of politics and power ranges from creating a more effective global infrastructure for the exchange of ideas, products, services, and money, to a singular authoritarian government made of international bankers and intellectual elite. The benefits of globalization are worth exploring, but whenever decisions are made behind closed doors without informing the public, it is rarely in the interests of the public. Every citizen should know what the ruling class thinks and how they plan to govern us if we are to keep our democracy strong.

The Central Intelligence Agency

The Central Intelligence Agency (CIA) is a civilian intelligence agency of the United States government that reports to the director of national intelligence; it is responsible for providing national security intelligence to senior policy makers and engages in covert activities at the request of the president of the United States. The CIA employs an estimated 20,000 people, most of which gather and analyze political and economic data from around the world. Relatively few CIA employees work in covert operations or spying.

The CIA was created by Congress with the passage of the National Security Act of 1947 and signed into law by President Harry Truman. It replaced the Office of Strategic Services (OSS) used for intelligence gathering in World War II. Founding members of the CIA include Allen Dulles and his brother John Foster Dulles, Prescott Bush (father of President George Bush, Sr.), and Rear Admiral Roscoe H. Hillenkoetter who was appointed its first director. Hillenkoetter worked in intelligence with Rockefeller in Paris during World War II. Both Allen Dulles and John Foster Dulles were close friends with the Rockefeller family. The Bush family has been friends and business partners with the Rockefellers for four generations; moreover, the original offices of the this intelligence organization during World War II were in room 3603 in Rockefeller Center, just down from the Rockefeller's own offices; the Rockefellers also hosted the CIA office at the World Trade Center building seven before it was demolished on 9/11.

During World War II, David Rockefeller served in North Africa and France for military intelligence and set up political and economic intelligence units, and later served as an assistant military attaché at the American Embassy in Paris. Although the Rockefellers are not officially mentioned as working for the CIA (they don't tend to release such information), several people who have worked for the Rockefellers have become the CIA's director. Allen Dulles was a close personal friend of the Rockefeller family and former director of the J. Henry Schroder bank (one of the largest asset managers in the United Kingdom and associated with the royal family's finances) which Avery Rockefeller was a partner of and which was later sold to Rockefeller's Citigroup. Brother John Foster Dulles is an in-law of the Rockefellers and their families share common interests in banking and other industries.

In Cary Reich's biography of David's brother Nelson, she claims that David was regularly briefed on covert intelligence operations at the direction of Allen Dulles. The people at the top of America's intelligence are families that have known each other for many years and these families have intermarried and have share common business interests and globalist worldviews. This knowledge will explain many of the CIA's more controversial incidents, and the underlying reason for so many of our wars.

Whereas the CIA plays an important role in maintaining the peace, and most of those who work for the agency (the Company) deserve our respect and appreciation, those at the top have repeatedly used the CIA to serve corporate interests and personal political advantage, and in so doing committed acts that are both against our own laws and the will of the people. In order to improve our government, our intelligence network, and reestablish credibility around the world all, citizens, particularly Americans, should know how the United States has been involved in immoral and unethical acts, most of which are kept from the American people. The following examples are only the tip of the iceberg, and the only ones appropriate to write about publically since these incidents have already been covered in the press and our discussing them publically is no longer a threat to our national security. Moreover, the following examples have been confirmed by Directors of the CIA or disclosed in public testimony before Congress, although many of the details are still in dispute.

In 1948 the CIA created its covert action wing called the **Office of Policy Coordination** (OPC), led by leading Wall Street lawyer Frank Wisner, and George Kennan, for "covert psychological operations, propaganda and paramilitary training" (NSC 10/2). It's reported (but not verified) responsibilities included "propaganda, economic warfare, preventive direct action, including sabotage, antisabotage, demolition and evacuation procedures, subversion against hostile states, including assistance to underground resistance groups, and support of indigenous anticommunist elements in threatened countries of the free world." In 1949 the CIA creates its first of many propaganda outlets, **Radio Free Europe**, which both helped Soviet-bloc nations gain the Western perspective of world events and encouraged democratic movements, but it also had quite a reputation for broadcasting outright false information too. At one time it was actually against the law to publish in the American media what was being transmitted abroad. Radio Free Europe was supported by an organization called the Crusade for Freedom, and future president Ronald Reagan served as their spokesman on television.

Later in the 1940s the CIA began **Operation Mockingbird**, recruiting the assistance of American and other news agencies to spy and disseminate propaganda on behalf of the CIA. Frank Wisner, Allan Dulles, Richard Helms, and Philip Graham (who was also the publisher of the *Washington Post*) led this program, which included ABC, NBC, CBS, *Time*, *Newsweek*, Associated Press, United Press International, Reuters, Hearst Newspapers, Scripps-Howard, Copley News Service, and others. By the CIA's own admission, at least twenty-five organizations and 400 journalists became CIA assets. For instance, Prescott Bush served on the Board of CBS News for many years, and most major news agencies have representation from the intelligence community on their boards or in executive positions. Most of our leading publishers of news are also members of the Council on Foreign Relations.

All news coming to the networks is scrubbed before being presented to broadcasters. They decide who is a freedom fighter or a terrorist, who is a friend of the United States and who is not, what Americas interests are, and what you will think, what opinions you form, and what perceptions of the world you hold. Typically, agencies that collect news at the wholesale level, organizations like United Press International, Associated Press and Reuters, provide local broadcasters the news and the local stations package it in a form that appeals to their listeners regionally. Most of the critical information and facts that would advise a citizen of what is really going on is never (rarely) relayed to the public, and on occasions when information does get leaked it is typically covered up, or the CIA creates a conspiracy theory so crazy and absurd that any legitimate information gets clumped in the "crazy file" of the public's mind. If information gets labeled conspiracy, we are conditioned to reject it as long as the source appears to be credible, like the news. As a result, Americans are amongst the least informed on global events of all the industrialized nations, including the actions of its own government or intelligence agencies.

Moreover, almost all radio in America is now controlled by one conglomerate called Clear Channel, which packages the news. It was shortly after this monopoly was formed that dozens of politically oriented radio shows started entering the airwaves and promoting particular political agendas that just happen to be the same as the cartel and they have created the appearance of the left and right in a battle that grips the nation. Originally broadcasters received their licenses on the condition of providing news as a service to the public. Years of lobbying have loosened those restrictions and most news broadcasts are more a form of infotainment, presenting more opinions and editorial rhetoric than objective news or even thorough coverage of world affairs. Now the news is mostly spin or propaganda, and most people are either on one side or the other. That's a device used by propagandists to control people.

The American public is rarely informed about what is really going on, our broadcasting is spun to entertain and direct you to think in a way that serves Americans' interests best. To do this the information is made to bring up strong emotions rather than rational debate. Once you get agitated and angry, you become vulnerable and suggestible; it's literally a shift in consciousness, as if you've been hypnotized. Once your brain is wired in, you become easy to manipulate. Public Relations is a multibillion dollar industry. The programming is designed to create a "manufactured consent" that we are trained to go along with. What you want to buy, where you want to go, what you think, and your very perceptions are molded by a system that is updated and modified continuously. We think what we are directed to think by design. We live in a world of manufactured consent.

In 1953 the CIA sponsored operation **MK-ULTRA**, funded in part by the Rockefeller and Ford Foundations, to research propaganda, brainwashing, public relations, advertising, hypnosis, and other forms of mind control. In the media every color, image, sound, choice of words, and inflections you see, hear, or feel, are designed for you to think and emote without consciously knowing what ideas and feelings you are process- ing. It's not a conspiracy; it's simply how they get you to watch and spend money or do whatever they want another or society to think, or do. According to studies, we believe whatever we hear most often. Before you buy almost anything, the sug- gestion to buy it was already in your head, and your every thought was introduced to you by another. Most people are not conscious of what they are thinking; they are relatively unconscious.

Within the United States Homeland Security infrastructure lies an organization called the **National Security Agency** (NSA); as it is a secret organization little information is available, but their main facility has over 18,000 parking spaces, which gives you an idea of how many people work there. They use the Narus Insight System (STA 6400), an advanced software, as well as other types, to monitor billions of pieces of digital data per second; all satellite, cell, and Internet traffic around the world is monitored by the United States government in the name of stopping terrorism. All calls, all Web site visits, instant messaging, banking, and credit card transactions are now monitored by the government. In a recent court hearing that went over this new technology it was stated "It could go through all the information in all the books in the Library of Congress in a little over fifteen minutes." Attorney General Alberto Gonzales confirmed the existence of the program that was first reported by the *New York Times* in 2005. In 2008 the nation's telecommunications companies were given legal immunity for eavesdropping, according to testimony by Attorney General Eric Holder. Moreover, under the new USA Patriot Act, continued by President Barak Obama, the section entitled *Enhanced Surveillance Procedures* states:

> Notwithstanding any other law, the President, through the Attorney General, may authorize electronic

surveillance without a court order under this subchapter to acquire foreign intelligence information for a period not to exceed fifteen calendar days following a declaration of war by the Congress.

The CIA has also been involved in the overthrow of many democratically elected national leaders (by the CIA's own admission), but most of these overthrows were for economic advantage of corporate special interests and not for the national security of the United States. One of the best examples is **Guatemala** in 1954. When the democratically elected Jacob Arbenz proposed to nationalize the Rockefeller owned United Fruit Company (CIA Director Allen Dulles also owned stock), Arbenz was replaced with a right-wing dictator who ruthlessly ruled for the next forty years. Over 100,000 Guatemalans died in this CIA-backed military coup. This is no secret in Guatemala, but very few Americans ever knew. The news didn't cover it. It was all over Latin America, but Americans were ignorant of it and most still are.

After several CIA attempts to assassinate Fidel Castro failed, and learning that **Cuba** had Soviet medium range nuclear missiles, the CIA first trains Cuban exiles to fight and then leads an invasion force without President Kennedy's approval. Many leaders in the military, and the cartel, felt an invasion was needed to stop Castro before he could arm and launch his missiles, or threaten to do so. President Kennedy was trying to negotiate with Castro and the Soviet Union's leader Khrushchev. The CIA, CFR, and the cartel thought Kennedy was being weak on communism. When Kennedy woke up and learned that Operation Mongoose, the invasion of 1,500 troops, had already begun, he called the Air Force and recalled the American planes that were to provide air support, and, as a result, those Cuban solders landing on the beach of the Bay of Pigs were decimated. Kennedy had egg on his face, and a lot of leaders within government were angry with him, as he was with them.

As a consequence, Kennedy fired CIA director Allen Dulles (who, ironically, later led the Warren investigation into the assassination of John F. Kennedy). Kennedy was able to assure the Soviet Union and Castro that the United States would not invade Cuba and would remove the nuclear missiles it placed in Turkey, which were pointed at Moscow, if the Soviet Union would withdraw their missiles, which they did, and war was avoided.

In later interviews, leading Soviet generals who were in Cuba at the time, confirmed that those nuclear missiles were armed and already targeted for Washington, New York, Miami, and other key cities on the Eastern Seaboard. Castro had stated publically on several occasions that if the invasion had proceeded, and if Kennedy had not called, he would have definitely launched those missiles, even if it meant the United States retaliated and destroyed Cuba. The Soviet leaders confirmed this intention. We nearly started a nuclear war because of the misguided actions of those at the highest levels of the CIA who thought they knew better and were above the law and our government. This is a recurring theme between our Congress and the higher elite level of government or the cartel of government. This is why more Congressional oversight is needed; the decision to go to war should be agreed on by informed citizens, and their elected representatives.

The Assassination of John F. Kennedy

President John F. Kennedy (1953-1960) comes from a family that was not as aligned with the cartel or the Council on Foreign Relations, he was from another American royal family and didn't trust the New York bankers. He also had a different worldview, as the Bay of Pigs incident indicates. He had just fired the CIA director Dulles and had a bill ready to break up the CIA and give intelligence gathering back to the military like it was before the war. He also had Executive Order 11110 that would give the U.S. Treasury the power to issue money again— Silver certificates—a brilliant idea. This was a direct threat to the cartel and its Federal Reserve, and thus threatening the dominant power paradigm in America.

In a landmark case that went to an appellate court, *E. Howard Hunt* vs. *Liberty Lobby the Spotlight Newspaper*, former CIA agent Victor Marchetti tells the *Spotlight* newspaper that CIA agent E. Howard Hunt was involved in the assassination of President Kennedy. Hunt had just been busted for illegally breaking into the Watergate Hotel and illegally wiretapping the Democratic convention for President Richard Nixon, but he still sues the *Spotlight* for defamation. Originally Hunt won the case because he was able to get a judge who would not admit any evidence to support the fact that he might actually be involved in the assassination. On appeal, Mark Lane, who was a prominent Washington lawyer, leader in the Democratic party and best-selling author of *Rush to Judgment*, which questioned the Warren Commission's conclusion that a single gunman killed the president, is able to depose several directors of the CIA and come up with enough evidence to show that E. Howard Hunt was in fact involved or appeared to be, so that the jury overturned the defamation verdict. This is all explained in Mark's book *Plausible Denial*. Mark explains that after the trial the press was told not to cover it for threat of losing their license to broadcast; not one network would cover one of the most important trials of the century, for fear of reprisal of our government—the cartel.

In 1976 the United States House of Representatives Select Committee on Assassinations (HSCA) was established to investigate the John F. Kennedy assassination and the Martin Luther King, Jr. assassination and the shooting of Governor Wallace. In 1979, after reviewing all the facts, this bipartisan committee concluded that John F. Kennedy was very likely assassinated as a result of a conspiracy and not one man acting alone, and they ruled out the Soviet Union, Cuba, anti-Castro groups, or organized crime as the leader, and accused the CIA of withholding requested information and even obstruction of justice.

The Committee also learned that the CIA's special liaison to the committee researchers, George Joannides was actually involved with some of the organizations that Lee Harvey Oswald was involved with in the months leading up to the assassination, including the DRE an anti-Castro group supported by the CIA where Joannides worked in 1963. Thus, Lee Harvey Oswald worked for a CIA front group; it was also discovered that Oswald had learned to speak Russian in the United States Army Intelligence. Moreover, the committee also concluded "there is a likelihood" that this was the result of a conspiracy, but stopped short of implicating any government agency.

The Department of Justice, FBI, CIA, and the Warren Commission were all criticized for not revealing all the information needed or requested in 1964; they were accused of stalling and refusing to provide the documentation subpoenaed, and not remembering a lot when asked the most compromising questions. Interestingly, the Warren Commission, which was the first group to investigate the assassination, was comprised mostly of people who Kennedy had fired or was going to fire and those who had the most to lose from his new executive orders; all the findings from the Warren investigation are sealed and hidden from the public. So far, all the evidence released through the Freedom of Information Act demonstrates that the conclusions of the Warren investigation were wrong. The only congressman to petition the Congress to reopen the Warren investigation so the public may learn all the facts, Allard Lowinstein from New York, was shot in the forehead at his office. Allard suspected that he might get killed for continuing to petition the re-opening of the Warren investigation, he told this author as much just months before it happened. He also thought the CIA would be involved.

The committee also concluded that the Secret Service was deficient in their protection of the president. The day Kennedy arrived in Dallas, Texas, the secret service reduced their security force. If you watch the Zapruder film (on YouTube) in slow motion you can clearly see that the secret service agents assigned to protect the president are recalled from their positions surrounding the limo the president was traveling in, just seconds before the shooting, by what we are told are CIA agents in the car behind the president—the agents are called back as if to make room for the gunman (a hand motion waving the others to fall back, and them leaving the car is clearly seen). Moreover, in slow motion it is very clear to see bullets from different directions hit the president. Dozens of people who have come forth to provide more information or testify have disappeared or suddenly and mysteriously died - over thirty. Witnesses who were interviewed tell us that the federal agents conducting the interviews told them what to say or not say and threatened not to say things like hearing second gunshots. Moreover, Army intelligence officer James Powell and mafia hit-man Jim Bandon a.k.a. Eugene Brading were also identified by Dallas police as being in the Dallas Book Depository (TSBD) building at the time of the shooting, but they were released without further questioning, and their presence was never questioned during the Warren investigation. During the Clay Shaw trial in 1969, prosecutor Jim Garrison tried to extradite Brading from California, but then Governor Ronald Reagan refused to comply.

Before his death, former CIA operative E. Howard Hunt, discussed his knowledge of and participation in the plot to kill John F. Kennedy in several audio and video testimonies he gave to his son, Saint John Hunt, shortly before his death (released in 2007). In his confession, which is preserved in his own voice and handwriting, Hunt also implicates then Vice

President Lyndon Johnson and CIA operatives Cord Meyer, Frank Sturgis, William K. Harvey, and David Sanchez Morales to carry out the plot; Hunt admitted to hearing of the plot ahead of time, clearly identifies the assassination as a CIA job, using the same foreign shooters the CIA had used on other government leaders such as Guatemala and attempted on Fidel Castro. Moreover, Hunt's family knew he was in Dallas at the time of the shooting, witnesses identify him being there giving money to CIA handler Frank Sturgis, and was further recognized in photos as being one of the "tramps" (in disguise) by his family.

The same thing happened with Bobby Kennedy, as with JFK, the day he was shot some of the same CIA operatives implicated in the JFK assassination were also present at the Ambassador Hotel on June 5th, 1968; the CIA was, again, accused of withholding needed information in the investigation, and again most of documents are either sealed or destroyed. In a broadcast and an article from the BBC news dated November 21, 2006, reporters claim that in an interview with David Morales, the former CIA chief of operations, said, "I was in Dallas when we got the son of a bitch, and I was in Los Angeles when we got the little bastard." (Referring to first John Kennedy and then his brother Bobby, who was assassinated in Los Angeles.) Yet no senator or congressman will reopen the investigation to determine who did it, because the truth is all the people on top already know, and they think it's best the public didn't know. Is that what is best? Who decides?

Multinational Espionage

From 1961 to 1969, the CIA was implicated in, or admitted to, leading assassinations and/or overthrows of other heads of government and putting in puppet governments: in the Dominican Republic (thrice), Ecuador (twice), Congo (twice),

Brazil, Indonesia, Greece, Bolivia and Uruguay. These vassals of the CIA are referred to as **Banana Republics** in the press. During the early 1970s the CIA was involved in overthrows in Cambodia, Laos, and Vietnam. The Vietnam War is commonly referred to in the United States government as the "CIA's war" because they planned and directed it; they have also been implicated in being involved in trafficking opium from the golden triangle (northern boarders of Vietnam, Laos and Cambodia), and more recently in Afghanistan among the Northern alliance who have worked with the CIA for years fighting Taliban. Afghanistan is believed to be the largest grower of Opium in the world now, and even they attribute much of their success to the CIA.

In most Third World (lesser developed) countries, the land and resources of a nation are owned or controlled by a handful of families—dictators who worked with the American corporations developing the countries resources—and during the 1960s many of the citizens of these countries were seeking freedom, rights and wanting to also benefit from their nations national resources; when a leader comes to upset that relationship they are taken out one way or the other. Typically these freedom movements and their leaders are labeled communist, and most do get their weapons from communist countries— it's a business. Most people in these little countries don't even know what communism is. They are just told things are going to get better if you elect us or fight for us; these wars are not fought over political ideology, they are fought over money and resources. Religion is used to incite, and ethnicity is used to divide; war is how conquest and money are made.

During the **Vietnam War** (1955-1975) American soldiers were originally sent to advise and train the South Vietnamese army to fight the North Vietnamese army, who were seeking liberation from the French, who tried to assume control of this former colony after the Japanese were defeated in WWII. The leader of North Vietnam, Ho Chi Minh, had lived in

New York and Boston from around 1912 to 1918 and said that his inspiration to lead Vietnam into independence came, in part, from listening to Marcus Garvey, a leading black civil rights leader. He also worked with the Allies in World War II serving as a spy for the OSS (CIA) to rid Indochina of the Japanese; originally Ho sought support from America, and when he realized that America was not going to help them, he turned to the Russians and the Chinese for military and economic aid and that's when the United States jumped in.

After the Korean War, the American government was keen to stop the spread of communism, and they implemented a policy of containment to keep communism from spreading throughout Asia—what they called the domino effect. On August 2, 1964, in what is called the **Gulf of Tonkin** incident, the destroyer USS *Maddox* was performing a DESOTO patrol, which involves ships patrolling hostile areas to gather data from sophisticated electronic eavesdropping equipment, when they were engaged by North Vietnamese torpedo boats trying to chase them out of their waters and they managed to do some slight damage to the destroyer and an aircraft.

Two days later the *Maddox* reported another engagement, but that report turned out to be false. However, this second incidence was used by President Lyndon Johnson to send the first combat troops into Vietnam. In an interview with the Secretary of Defense Robert McNamara years later, he claimed that the misinformation about what happened in the gulf was due to inaccurate information coming from the CIA that was briefing him; the implication was they misrepresented or distorted the perception to precipitate war. Apparently the reports were modified by the CIA before getting to the president to review. In 1965, President Johnson commented about the Gulf of Tonkin incident, saying: "For all I know, our navy was shooting at whales out there." They were just looking for any excuse to sell war to the American people; it was the propaganda needed to send American troops into Vietnam.

In 1967 the CIA coordinated with the South Vietnamese government in **Operation Phoenix**, which was an attempt to find and assassinate North Vietnamese insurgents operating in South Vietnam. According to a 1971 congressional report, this operation killed (without trial) over 20,000 people, including women and children. In 1963 the United States government began discussing the possibility of replacing South Vietnamese President Diem with another more willing to adhere to U.S. policy; Diem had begun discussing a unification with the North, and so he was assassinated in 1963.

Under the presidency of Richard Nixon (1969-1974) the war in Vietnam escalated; The National Security Council recommended a three-stage escalation of bombing in North Vietnam: Operation Flaming Dart, Operation Rolling Thunder, and Operation Arc Light. Between March 1965 and November 1968 operation Rolling Thunder alone dropped over a million tons of bombs, missiles, and rockets, more than was dropped by the Allies in all of World War II. It did nothing significant militarily, and it mostly killed civilians. It also crossed over into Laos and Cambodia. On the day that Richard Nixon and Secretary of State Henry Kissinger publically stated that the United States was not bombing other countries, specifically Laos and Cambodia, they knowingly were. Presidents routinely lie to the public about international and domestic events, and this problem is at the heart of why we are governed so poorly. The antiwar protests of the 1970s eventually led Nixon to end the war, and Saigon fell in 1975. It was the people standing up against the war, protesting, singing, defying, and resisting that made that shift in consciousness possible. The right to demonstrate is one of the most important rights Americans need to maintain.

Beginning in 1968 under the Johnson Administration the CIA began a program of spying on American citizens called **Operation Chaos**. The stated purpose was to go undercover as student radicals to spy on and disrupt campus organizations and protests of the Vietnam War or for civil rights demonstrations. Under the CIA's Office of Security over 7,000 individuals and 1,000 organizations were tracked. These covert activities included reading correspondence passing between the United States and the Soviet Union, infiltrating domestic antiwar and radical organizations (Project Merrimac), and work with college administrators and police in identifying antiwar activists and leaders in the women's liberation movement.

The response to the public outcry when this was finally revealed was to create the commission on CIA Activities within the United States, better known as the **Rockefeller Commission**, which was led by Nelson Rockefeller, then vice resident under Gerald Ford. Five of the eight members of the committee were members of the Council on Foreign Relations. Speaking of the Rockefeller Commission, then Deputy White House Chief of Staff Dick Cheney, who was a part of the commission, said it was to avoid "congressional efforts to further encroach on the executive branch." So you have the very people who are instigating these deeds heading up the commission to oversee if there was any wrongdoing by them? Today the National Security Agency (NSA) screens (listens electronically) to all forms of digital or analog communications of its citizens, including cell and Internet transmissions, in an effort to thwart extremists (Islamic or otherwise). We do not have privacy through any electronic means throughout this world.

The **Watergate** break-in of 1972 involved illegal wiretapping of the Democratic offices at the Watergate Hotel in Washington, DC. President Nixon sent a team of CIA operatives, including James McCord, E. Howard Hunt, and G. Gordon Liddy. These activities were organized and funded by a CIA front, the Mullen Company, a public relations firm. In a report by Howard Baker, the Republican vice chairman for the Watergate committee "The Mullen and Company has maintained a relationship with the Central Intelligence Agency since its incorporation in 1959." Throughout the Watergate hearing the CIA repeatedly refused to cooperate in supplying the requested information, and this lack of cooperation with the Congress in hearings is a recurring problem with the CIA and in our democracy. As a result of these investigations, the Watergate hearings, president Richard Nixon was impeached.

The nation of **Chile** has some of the largest copper and gold reserves in the world; mined by American/European mining companies the majority of the income made from the development of those resources typically goes to a handful of government, military, and business officials and little makes its way to programs that support the people. So, it is common for populist leaders to want to take the ownership of the nation's resources away from those powerful few and share those resources with the nation. This was the case with Latin America's first democratically elected leader Salvador Allende. Allende wanted to nationalize the American-owned mining companies and place them under the management of the government of Chile.

Now, it's important to understand that the two biggest mining companies in Chile were Anaconda Copper Company and Kennecott Copper Corporation. Anaconda is partially owned by the Rothschild consortium and by William Rockefeller (John's brother), and the funding was made through the National City Bank of New York and Standard Oil, also a Rockefeller holdings. Kennecott Copper is a division of Rio Tinto Group, a Rothschild holding, which was later acquired by Standard Oil of Ohio (SOHIO), and now BP is a major owner. It's all one consortium.

In 1973 the CIA supported a coup that puts General Augusto Pinochet in power, which saved their mining interests, but they put Pinochet, a vicious dictator in Allende's place. In 2000 the CIA released a report titled "CIA Activities in Chile" that revealed the CIA involvement before, during, and after the coup. In a money laundering case involving Pinochet and the Riggs Bank in Washington, Senator Coleman noted:

> This is sad, sordid tale of money laundering involving Pinochet accounts at multiple financial institutions using alias names, offshore accounts, and close associates. As a former General and President of Chile, Pinochet was a well-known human rights violator and violent dictator.

By the end of 1974 former CIA Director Richard Helms and James Angleton, the CIA's chief of counterintelligence, were both fired by the Congress for illegal activities. Later that same year Congress passed the Hughes Ryan Act, an amendment requiring the president to report non-intelligence CIA operations to the relevant congressional committees in a timely fashion.

The CIA was also involved in toppling the democratically elected progressive prime minister of **Australia**, Edward Whitlam, in 1979. It turns out the United States has a nuclear submarine base in western Australia that Whitlam wanted to close, and he wanted to make other reforms that the United States government did not believe were in its best interest. To accomplish this the CIA worked with Australia's governor general, a nonelected post assigned by the Queen of England, to dissolve the Whitlam government. The CIA also started a secret war in Angola that same year, and every press in the world covered it but the United States.

In 1979 the Soviet Union invaded and deployed troops into **Afghanistan**, and the United States began directing and funding the Mujahedeen to fight the Soviet Union; they even created a training base for them called al-Qaeda, which means the foundation or base. The United States, through the CIA, armed and trained el Qaeda; moreover the CIA funded and directed this war in secret, which is at the heart of so many political problems in the world today. This story is told in the popular movie *Charlie Wilson's War* starring Tom Hanks. During this period CIA agents and special forces servicemen began training these rebels, whose leader was Osama bin Laden, the son of one of Saudi Arabia's wealthiest family and friends to the Saudi royal family and the Bushes.

In the September 11, 2001 attacks, Brzezinski, former National Security Advisor to President Jimmy Carter, was criticized for his role in forming the Taliban and al Qaeda, which he has publically stated he planned with Carter to fight the Russians, without the American public knowing. How many American's know that our own government helped create al Qaeda, or supported and worked with Osama Bin Laden?

Originally Bin Laden was an asset of the CIA and we worked with him and trained him to fight the Soviets. After the September 11th attack television host Larry King interviewed Saudi Arabia's ambassador to the United States, Prince Bandar bin Sultan, on the Larry King Live show on national television.

During the questioning Larry, knowing Prince Bandar is friends with the bin Laden family, asked him if he has ever met and spoken with Osama bin Laden personally. The Prince replied, "Yes, only once, several years ago." Larry then asked what did he have to say to you? To which the Prince replied:

> This is ironic. He said to tell the Americans he appreciates the support in Afghanistan fighting the godless Russians. He came to thank me for my efforts to bring the Americans in. (cut to commercial).

Iran Contra Affair

In 1981, as vice president under Ronald Regan, George Bush, Sr. is elected leader of the newly created Crises Management staff of the National Security Council, overseeing covert operations (he had formally been director of the CIA). In 1982 Reagan creates the Standing Crisis Preplanning Group to train Sandinistas (exiled Nicaraguans) to subvert and attack the newly elected president of Nicaragua, who wanted to nationalize the oil reserves. So, Reagan picks Vice President Bush, who has already served as head of the CIA as its director. Bush then hires Colonel Oliver North, a black op's specialist, to assist him, as well as ex-CIA associates Donald Grace and Felix Rodriguez. In December of that same year the Congress passed the **Boland Amendment** forbidding the training, arming, or supporting the Sandinistas. So the National Security Council (NSC) creates another entity called the Smith Richardson Foundation, which first raises millions of dollars in the private sector, including oil money, and then sends those millions to the Sandinistas, subverting the intention of the Boland amendment that was passed as law.

The National Security Planning Group, also headed up by Bush Sr., was then created to discuss other ways to support the Sandinistas, and their (Bush's) suggestion was to sell missiles to Israel and have them send those millions in payment to the Sandinistas. According to National Security Advisor Robert McFarlane, who was there, Vice President Bush, CIA Director Cassey, and President Reagan all said yes to the idea, but Secretary of State Shultz and Secretary of Defense Weinberger said no. Next, getting wind of this covert action, the congress passed the **Bolan Amendment II** (1984) "clarifying" that the United States is to have no direct or indirect involvement with supporting the Sandinistas in any way. As history shows, they ignored the law and sent money and arms anyway. Their loyalty was to the elite they served, not the will and the law of the people.

Some of the findings of the Iran Contra investigation include: Charles Allen's (CIA) statement that "the Iranian Parliament had been discussing how George Bush is orchestrating a U.S. initiative to sell arms to Iran to gain release of the American hostages" (1985). In 1986 Amiran Nir, head of Israeli counter intelligence, meets with Oliver North in Israel to discuss selling arms to Iran for hostages, shortly thereafter Nir comes to Washington to meet with Oliver North and Admiral Poindexter.

The next day Secretary of Defense Casper Weinberger directs General Colin Powel to ship Tow antitank missiles to Iran, breaking the law. They thought they were above it, and they were downright smug testifying at the hearings. They resented us for even questioning them. They lie, they deny, they simply defy the Congress and the law to be true to the elite—the cartel. It's a state of consciousness, they are indoctrinated into a belief system that has manufactured a consent amongst its members; it's a manufactured state of mind, a mental conditioning, and those in it rarely even realize they are being played. Most citizens in our democracy are oblivious and ignorant of what's really going on in the world, and don't really care. Apathy is created by design. This is a curse to our culture that all citizens need to address.

This next piece of information is among the most telling. George W. Bush, then an oilman and later president, purchases a controlling interest in the **Harken Oil Company** and becomes its CEO. After taking control of the board of directors, as the majority stockholder, he brings on Sheik Abdullah Bakhash from the BCCI bank (world's largest bank for arms deals, drug trafficking, money laundering, and a CIA asset) to the board of directors. What very few people remember from the Iran-Contra hearings is that it was a Harken Oil Company tanker that shipped those missiles illegally to Iran while George Bush Jr. was its CEO and the majority owner of the company. This makes him culpable even if he didn't know, and obviously his dad, Bush Senior knew since he was Reagan's point man on this specific operation. But when any information came up regarding the Bushes or their assets, the meeting went behind closed doors. There is a level of government that our own

Congress cannot touch, and we are told it's in the interest of national security.

It is implausible that the CEO of a company wouldn't know missiles were on board his own ship, particularly when his father headed up the Security Planning Group that suggested the idea. Both George Bush Sr. and George Bush Jr. willfully defied the law explicitly stating that: 1) there is to be no arms for hostages trading and 2) no money is to go to the Sandinistas. Both Bushes used the Secrecy Act to protect themselves from testifying about these key areas, and the CIA was very uncooperative during the hearings, yet again. Both future presidents lied publically, stating that they knew nothing about it, when they were clearly actively involved. Most of the records have been sealed or were destroyed when George Bush Sr. became president, but National Public Radio broadcast and recorded the whole hearing, and this author heard it live himself. It is important to make particular note that those testifying, who willfully violated the Boland amendment and the express will of the people, were righteous and indignant about what they did. Each clearly expressed that their laws and rules trumped those of the law of the people and their true loyalty was for their inner circle, the cartel.

George Bush's Harkin Oil then becomes very active in developing oil in the Persian Gulf with the help of his father, who is now president of the United States. During the period of 1988-1990 the oil rich Gulf nation of **Bahrain** broke off negotiations with giant Amoco Oil to give exclusive rights to explore for gas and oil off the shores of Bahrain to Harken Oil. At the same time Bahrain was chosen by President Bush as the base to support our fleet in the Gulf, a multibillion dollar contract. So, now, George Bush Sr. and George Bush Jr. lay claim to some of the largest known gas and oil fields in the world.

House of Bush

There are many historic U.S. political families that have had a significant impact on the politics and economics of the United States. Some have a geographical power base, such as the Kennedys in Massachusetts; the Long family with Louisiana; Roosevelt in New York; the Lees in Virginia; the Daleys in Illinois; the Muhlenbergs in Pennsylvania, or the Tafts in Ohio. We've recently had Udalls serving congress in Colorado and New Mexico, Browns in California, and the Rockefellers are well represented, too. The Bush family was originally from Ohio and Connecticut but are now more associated with Texas and Florida. What becomes even more interesting is to look at the relationships between each of the presidents of the United States.

According to leading experts, Genealogics and Roglo, we take a recent example of George H.W. Bush. He is fourth cousin five times removed of U.S. president Millard Fillmore, fifth cousin four times removed of U.S. president Franklin Pierce, seventh cousin four times removed of U.S. president Abraham Lincoln, sixth cousin three times removed of U.S. president Ulysses S. Grant, sixth cousin three times removed of U.S. president Rutherford B. Hays, fourth cousin three times removed of U.S. president James Garfield, seventh cousin twice removed of U.S. president Grover Cleveland, seventh cousin three times removed of U.S. president Theodore Roosevelt, sixth cousin three times removed of U.S. president Franklin D. Roosevelt, sixth cousin three times removed of U.S. president William Taft, tenth cousin of U.S. president Herbert Hoover, sixth cousin twice removed of U.S. president Richard Nixon, and seventh cousin of U.S. president Gerald Ford. This is America's royalty.

We begin our study of the Bush legacy four generations back to George W. Bush's great grandfather, Samuel Bush. The patriarchal succession goes as follows: Samuel Bush, Prescott

Bush, George H.W. Bush (Sr.), and George W. Bush (Jr.). The other important name to recognize is George Herbert Walker, whose daughter, Dorothy, married Prescott Bush, and gave the proud name Walker to their children. Understanding the in-law link pays a critical part in understanding the financial holdings and power base of these American royal families and their political and economic ties.

Samuel Bush (1863-1948) was a leading industrialist and banker, who was partners with Frank Rockefeller (John D. Rockefeller's brother) in Buckeye Steel Co. When Frank died Samuel became president. Buckeye was one of the major steel manufacturers providing steel for railroads and shipbuilding, and they were one of the largest manufacturers of shells for bullets (interests in Remington) and other armaments. Samuel Bush was also a partner in several railroad and oil companies with the Rockefellers. He worked for Harriman, one of the world's largest merchant bankers; he also served on the board of the Federal Reserve Board of Cleveland, and the Huntington National Bank of Columbus.

Samuel also served on the War Services Board during WWI, coordinating the development of our war industry to support the war. So, the Bush fortune and power base lies within the industries of steel, oil, armaments, shipping, and banking, and the Bush family's assets and business relationships are intertwined with those the Rockefeller, Walker, Harriman, and Morgan, and by them the Bank of England, royal money and the Rothschilds; these families are the most influential in the industries of oil, banking, arms manufacturing, and now in politics.

George Herbert Walker (1875-1953) was the founder and majority owner of H.G. Walker & Co., a leading International Banking conglomerate, primarily merchant banking (private money owning interest in companies it lends to). Herbie held major interests in American Shipping and Commerce, Union

Banking Company, and the Hamburg-American Line (the larg-est ship builders in the world based in Hamburg, Germany), as well as other holdings in railroads (e.g., Pacific Railroad), oil, and was partners with J.P. Morgan, another leading indus-trialist and bankers, as well as serving as president of W.A. Harriman's merchant banking company. So, the Walker fam-ily fortune is in banking, oil, shipbuilding, and manufactur-ing armaments, such as war ships used in World War I and II. Herbie's daughter, Dorothy, married Samuel Bush's son Prescott, and their son is George H.W. Bush (President Bush Sr.)

Averill Harriman (1891-1986) served as governor of New York, ambassador to the United Kingdom and Russia during WWII, and was secretary of commerce under Truman. He owed the largest merchant bank in America and was heavily invested in many industries, including Harriman Enterprises (the world's largest shipping line), Hamburg-American Line (along with Herbie Walker), Harriman Morton Shipping (with J.P. Morgan), and Walker-Harriman in Berlin (partners with Warburg Bank, one of the largest names in banking in Europe). He was director of Union Pacific Railroad, president of Southern Pacific Railroad, and owned part of Wells Fargo Bank. Harriman was also majority share holder of Harriman Fifteen Corporation, along with Walker and Bush, which owned a majority of Silesian Holdings that mined one-third of the coal and zinc mining operations in Germany, and produced most of the steel and armaments used in the both world wars.

In 1931 W.A. Harriman merged with Brown Brothers, who were the largest merchant (private) banking firm in the United Kingdom, personally managing the queen of England's finances, including Royal Dutch Shell oil company (which she owned jointly with Queen Beatrice of the Netherlands) to form the largest private merchant bank in the world: **Brown Brothers Harriman**. In 1942 Harriman partnered up with Fritz Thyssen to form the Union Banking Corporation, of which Prescott Bush became the director. The Thyssen family was one of the largest industrialists in Germany. Fritz controlled the German Steel Trust, which produced 50 percent of Germany's pig iron, and manufactured most of the materials Hitler used to build his war machine (they were forced to divest German assets at the onset of WWII). Fritz's other partner was Bush and Friedrick Flick, another large industrialist in Germany. So, the Harriman holdings include banking, oil, shipping, steel, armaments, and mining; they are all partners— a syndicate.

So, before we begin our study of Prescott Bush (Samuel's son, Herbie's Walker's son-in-law, and Harriman's employee and later partner) we see the Bush's fortune is tied to the industries of banking, oil, steel, armaments, shipping, and mining (as well as others), they are partners with the Rockefellers, Browns (and by them the queens of England and the Netherlands), the Thyssens and Flicks (largest industrialists in Germany), as well as J.P. Morgan, the Warburgs, and the Vanderbilts. The Bush family now plays a key role in the largest merchant banking (private investment) companies in the world and has major holdings in banking, oil, armaments, steel, shipping and mining, before either of America's future presidents were born.

Prescott Bush (1895-1972) was a U.S. Senator from Connecticut, a partner with Brown Brothers Harriman and Director of Herbie Walker's Union Banking Corp. of New York. Prescott worked in intelligence gathering during WWI, and was one of the principal founders of the CIA, and also directed investments with Brown Brothers Harriman. Prescott also served on the board of CBS broadcasting. Prescott married Dorothy Walker, daughter of Herbie Walker, and had five children: Prescott (Bushy) Bush, George Herbert Walker Bush (forty-first president), Nancy Bush, Jonathan Bush, and William (Bucky) Bush. Jonathan Bush ran the Riggs Bank, the largest bank in Washington DC, the only Federal Depository in Washington; this bank is famous for being used by ambassadors and for financing the telegraph and providing $7.2 million to the government for the purchase of Alaska, as well as being part of the Federal Reserve. William Bush was CEO of Bush O'Donnell & Co., an investment banking company working in the industries already mentioned. So, during the next generation, the Bush family fortune grew as the need for weapons, oil, and money grew. Prescott moved the family up into the next echelon of the global power base, and drew the family into the political arena. Being part of the founding of both the CIA and in the Federal Reserve, Bush becomes one of the most powerful names in America.

George Herbert Walker Bush (1924-present) served as Senator, Director of the CIA, Vice President, and then forty-first president of the United States. After serving as the youngest aviator in WWII, George H.W. Bush (Sr.) worked for the oil drilling company Dresser Industries, an investment of Brown Brothers Harriman (who both his father and father-in-law were partners). He later started Bush-Overby Oil (1951), and then Co-founded Zapata Petroleum Corp, with financial support from his grandfather George Herbert Walker, and started drilling in the Permian basin in Texas (1953). He was later named president of the Zapata Offshore Company, a subsidiary specializing in offshore drilling the following year (the name Zapata came from the movie *Viva Zapata* with Marlon Brando). In 1963 South Penn Oil, a Rockefeller holding, merged with Bush's Zapata Oil to become Pennzoil (*Penn*sylvania *Z*apata *Oil*). In 1964 Pennzoil was contracted to drill wells in Kuwait and is one of the largest producers in the Middle East. So, the Bushes have massive oil holdings in Kuwait, and one of its subsidiaries, Seacat-Zapata, was one of the largest drillers in the Persian Gulf.

Zapata Offshore concentrated its business in the Caribbean, Gulf of Mexico and Central American Coast including Nicaragua, and had several subsidiaries, including: Seacat-Zapata Offshore (Persian Gulf), Zapata de Mexico, Zapata International, Zapata Mining, Zavala Oil, Zapata Overseas and

41 percent of Amata Gas Corp. U.S. Army intelligence officer Brigadier General Russell Bowen states that Zapata Oil was a cover for CIA activities involving anti-Castro activities and in preparation for the Bay of Pigs invasion of Cuba. His father is one of the founders of the CIA. Zapata Offshore provided the use of two ships as cover in the Bay of Pigs invasion: The *Barbara J.* (the name of Bush's wife) and *Houston* (where Zapata was based). Allen Dulles, who served as director of the CIA, worked for the Rockefellers and was a close family friend of both the Bushes and Walkers, and coordinated the invasion. Even the CIA's codename for this operation was "Operation Zapata."

CIA liaison officer Col. L. Fletcher Prouty testifies that Operation Zapata utilized the Zapata Oil company ships and offshore oil drilling platforms in the operation. Moreover, former CIA Officers Robert T. Crowley and William Coroson mention that the CIA considered Bush an asset in an internal memo released in 2007, and J. Edgar Hoover, FBI Director, identifies George Bush as working for the CIA in a memo from 1963. Three of Bush's other partners in Zapata, Hugh Liedtke, Bill Liedtke, as well as Thomas J. Devine all had previously worked for the CIA. Officially, of course, the CIA denies any connection (which they must as it was a covert operation). Zapata's filing records with the U.S. Securities and Exchange Commission during those years of covert operations were destroyed shortly after Bush became vice president. Clearly Bush Sr. must have had some experience in working with intelligence with the CIA before becoming its director, and his involvement in covert operations plays a big part in our story.

George W. Bush started out after college as an oilman who got into politics with the support of the oil interests, including their own. The W in Bush's name stands for Walker, the in-law oil magnate. The Bush presidency is defined by the wars in Iraq and Afghanistan, and in securing Americas national interests. Iraq holds around 20 percent of the known petroleum reserves and is expected to have additional reserves yet untapped and Afghanistan is needed for a critical oil pipeline and to keep competing oil interests like Russia and China out as well as to put pressure on neighboring Iran.

Kuwait had originally been a part of what is now Iraq; the oil companies carved it out and supported the local tribal leader in return for oil concessions. Originally Iraq had been an ally of the United States, but when Saddam started letting the Russian and French oil companies in, and began trading in euros instead of dollars, he became our enemy. When George W. Bush invaded Iraq in the second Gulf War and took control of the country, one of the first things they did was seize control of all oil production, annulled all contracts with all other oil companies and gave it back to American and British companies, favoring those with whom the Bushes are partners.

After 9/11 **Richard Clark**, National Security Advisor, stated emphatically and with certainty that Iraq had nothing to do with 9/11 and that they had no capacity for making a nuclear bomb in the near future. He is on record as saying that upon hearing this, the president told him to find the evidence. Clark refused and was fired. The CIA is on record as stating that Iraq had nothing to do with 9/11 and the executive branch ignored all intelligence gathered by the CIA. CIA intelligence officers are on record as stating that they repeatedly tried to inform president of the facts and that he did not want to hear them and insisted that they keep looking for evidence in Iraq.

Interpol and the entire intelligence community of the world cited that there was absolutely no connection with Iraq and 9/11 and the United Nations inspectors who spent years investigating the nuclear capacity of Iraq stated with certainly that there was no evidence that Iraq had "yellow cake uranium" or the capacity to make nuclear weapons. All this information is available to the public. Yet President Bush, Vice President Cheney, and National Security Advisor and later Secretary of State Rice all claimed that Iraq did, or may shortly, have nuclear weapons on national news despite not having a single shred of evidence to support that claim, and being told quite the contrary by every expert and adviser in our government and outside it.

In February 2001, before 9/11, Colin Powel, then joint chief of staff of the United States military and later secretary of state under George W. Bush, stated "Saddam Hussein has no weapons of mass destruction," and in July of 2001 Condoleezza Rice, then national security advisor and later secretary of state after Colin Powell, also stated in July of 2001 "We are able to keep arms from him, his forces have not been rebuilt." However, after September 11th the rhetoric changed, and night after night Americans saw images of nuclear bombs going off when talking about Saddam and the need to take him out, and the United States press completely rolled over; we didn't receive accurate news, we received propaganda, and it led us into another war American's didn't want.

General **Colin Powel**, serving as secretary of state, who announced the "Yellow Cake uranium" intelligence at the United Nations assembly to gain support for the war, later admits that the evidence was weak and ultimately unfounded. Finally, the congressional bipartisan **9/11 Commission** report concluded that Iraq had nothing to do with 9/11. Yet this was the reason giving to the American people for going to war in Iraq. Essentially, the whole thing was trumped up to invade Iraq and seize control of their vast oil reserves. Saddam was clearly a vicious dictator, but all intelligence gathering from around the world, including our own, clearly showed that he placed no immediate threat to our national security or even Israel's. The Bush Administration gave millions of dollars to the Iraqi National Congress that supports both the American presence in Iraq and the development of their oil by American and British companies.

The leadership of Iraq and the companies that control its oil development are chosen by the American government. The current government in Iraq is a puppet of U.S. oil interests, not to say they are not getting more freedom too. Our presence there is to control the oil. The wars in Iraq are all about oil. Moreover, the people who brought us into war all have worked for the oil industry, banking, and defense contractors, and they all profit from the war. Moreover, the U.S. Defense Department is unable to properly account for $8.7 billion in Iraqi oil money tapped by the United States for rebuilding Iraq; that's not an accounting error, all money is tracked through the banking system. That money was stolen and now Americans have to pay that bill no matter who has the money or what it's being used for. Yet, those responsible have not been punished and the issue is left unresolved. Congress is impotent, the American people need to learn the facts and get involved because our representatives are not doing their job.

Dominant Global Military Presence

In order to both protect the homeland and secure America's national interests; as of March 2008, the United States maintains over 820 military bases in at least 135 countries. Currently (2011) America keeps some 1,084,548 personnel on active duty in the United States and its territories, and has another million or so in reserve. The United States also maintains bases in Europe (Germany, Greece, Italy, United Kingdom, Spain, Norway, Sweden, Belgium, Portugal, Netherlands, Greenland, France, Poland, Turkey, and Kosovo). In Asia and Oceania (South Korea, Japan, Philippines, Diego Garcia, Singapore, Thailand, Malaysia, Australia, Marshall Islands, and New Zealand), Latin America (Antigua, Saint Helena, Cuba, Netherlands Antilles, and Panama). Most of the military in Latin America studied in America. In Africa Dubouti, Kenya, Egypt, Sinai Desert and the United States is creating a whole military command for Africa—AfriCom—to protect the recent oil reserves discovered there. In the Middle East we have some 50,000 troops in Iraq and 98,000 in Afghanistan (August 2010), as well as bases in Qatar, Bahrain, Kuwait, Oman, and the United Arab Emirates. Almost the entire military of Israel is subsidized by the United States; the United States dominates the Middle East.

Military power: Brazil, France, India, Russia, Thailand, China, and the United Kingdom each have one small aircraft carrier, Italy and Spain each have two, but only America has supercarriers. The United States has eleven carriers, plus many other air transport ships, more powerful submarines, air power, and a large seasoned and a technically sophisticated army. With satellites and stealth technologies, the United States can drop a bomb on anyone anywhere and at anytime. Our intelligence network is in every country. We even have private armies, so the United States can deny involvement. The world has seen nothing like this. The United States is a stabilizing influence in the world, a strong ally to fight evil regimes, but all too often now the United States is also considered by much of the world as the Evil Empire, where a few rich control the world. It's the 1 percent verses the world in the minds of the masses—representative government verses the dark side.

The military is the arm of power, which is directed by money; whoever controls the money controls the power.

Oil Power

Standard Oil Company, established in 1870 by John D. Rockefeller, was the largest oil company in the world, controlling over 80 percent of the world's petroleum resources. In 1880 the congress passed the Sherman Antitrust Act to stop price fixing (driving the price up and keeping competition out) and Standard Oil was broken up into**: Exxon, Mobil, Socal, Chevron** (formally Chevron-Texaco), **Amoco, Atlantic Richfield (ARCO), Conoco-Philips, Esso,** and **South Penn Oil (Pennzoil)**, which later merged with Shell Oil.

Under the second Bush Administration these Rockefeller holdings were able to merge again creating an even stronger monopoly, and the price of oil again skyrocketed. The oil companies set the retail price of oil (petroleum products, such as, gasoline), a point overlooked by the press that focuses on crude oil prices as the culprit of high gasoline prices. Higher crude prices caused by increasing demand relative to supply, especially with China and India competing for crude, certainly drives prices up, but the other leading cause of higher gas prices is what the oil companies charge, and they charge whatever they want because there is no longer any competition. They are making a fortune on us, just look at their bottom line.

According to *Fortune* magazine's Global 500, ranking of the top 500 companies in the world, based on gross revenues and profits, five of the top ten companies in the world are oil companies. Each of these five companies (Exxon/Mobil, Royal Dutch Shell, BP, Chevron, and Conoco-Philips) each receives more in annual revenues than 90 percent of the countries in the world. Once this Rockefeller Exxon/Mobil-Chevron-Conoco-Philips monopoly was established through the Bush Administration each of the oil companies in this monopoly started recording record profits. In 2007 Chevron posted record profits for the fourth straight year, earning $18.7 billion. Exxon/Mobil, the world's largest oil company made a new world record by posting a $40.6 billion profit in 2007. Exxon/Mobil's revenues of $404 billion exceed the gross domestic product (GDP) of over 120 countries. So, yes, part of your higher gas prices are due to increased demand relative to lagging supply pushing up the price of crude oil, but a very large percentage comes from gouging from the oil monopoly which is clearly shown in, refining costs and the increased profits of the oil companies. They charge you more, and they make more profit. High oil prices are one of the leading causes of inflation, so these higher gas prices were a major contributing factor leading us into this depression (2011).

Increased transportation costs affect the cost of almost all goods. Higher energy costs drive up the costs of manufacturing and drives our utility costs up. The whole economy is negatively affected. Automobile sales go down and manufacturers have to lay off employees and our unemployment rate goes up. Plus our national debt goes up to pay for protecting those oil assets and increased government deficit spending, which further weakened our economy. It's a deliberate downward spiral, technically, it's called a "death spiral," and it's used frequently. The oil monopoly has brought the entire country to its knees; they can turn it on or off and we are as dependent on them as we are the banking system.

Moreover, the assets of the Rockefeller conglomerate **Exxon-Mobil- Chevron-Conoco-Phillips** total more than double the next largest conglomerate, Wall-Mart Stores. There has never been as large or more powerful industrial entity in the world, aside from the money cartel itself. Only a hand full of countries, not companies but countries, have economies bigger than this conglomerate. Modern history, especially American, has been molded by our strategic objective of controlling the world oil supply. The National Security Council's stated objectives are to secure oil reserves as it is deemed critical in securing "America's national interests." During the Nixon years, while Henry Kissinger was head of the NSC and developing American foreign policy (which has not fundamentally changed since then), it was deemed in America's interest to gain control of "our" oil supplies around the world.

During the Ford years Nelson Rockefeller sat on the National Security Council and helped developed its strategic objects. We had two oil magnates as president. During the Bush administration we had the former CEO of an oil development company, with massive financial interests in oil as our vice president, Dick Cheney. The secretary of state and former national security advisor, Condoleezza Rice, used to sit on the board of Exxon, she's a stockholder and consultant, and even has a supertanker named after her. So the president, vice president, and secretary of state, and everyone who trumpeted the need to wage war on Iraq based on the false premises of the Iraqis being behind 9/11 and developing a nuclear capacity. All have, and do, profit from America taking control of Iraq's oil reserves. They are making money from the war in Iraq.

Global Politics

At the end of World War I, the Ottoman (Turks) controlled most of Arabia, Persia, and the Middle East. They sided with the Germans in World War I, who lost, and so lost control of the Middle East after the war. The British and Americans now had military control of the region, and British and American oil companies had recently discovered oil there and divided it up between them. The oil companies redrew the map of the Middle East and put local leaders in power in exchange for exclusive oil rights. The Turkish Petroleum Company (TPC, later known as IPC) originally had the monopoly on Mesopotamian oil. In what was known as the Red Line Agreement the Allied superpowers divided up of Middle East based on its oil. Kuwait, originally a part of Iraq, was carved out as a separate sovereignty as a concession to the British who were aware of the vast reserves under its soil (one of the biggest in the world). The small nations of Oman, Qatar, and Bahrain were also carved out and given sovereignty in return for granting American oil companies oil concessions. After World War II, British and American oil interests secured the remaining major oil reserves in the Middle East and British and American governments protected and installed their national leaders, mostly dictators, to secure their oil rights "in the interest of national security."

When Iran's democratically elected prime minister Mohammed Mosaddeq received the votes from his Parliament to nationalize the Iran oil reserves (to share the profits of oil with the people of Iran), that were controlled by British and American oil companies, the West reacted quickly and harshly. Hearing this, both British and American governments worked to overthrow Mosaddeq and install the Shah in what the CIA called **Operation Ajax**. It's well documented and not even denied by the CIA, which feels it was justified as it was deemed in America's best interest. However, it's the underlying reason for the revolution in Iran, too. The people of Iran certainly know the Shah was a puppet of America, directed by the CIA. The whole Middle East knows, and that's the fuel for terrorism. This American-led coup is resented by the people who want democracy like the United States has. The CIA's involvement was the very underpinning of outrage that led to the Revolution in Iran in the 1970s. The Shah, in turn, granted special oil concessions to British and American oil companies. The people who live in oil rich Middle Eastern countries all know that their leaders, all their leaders, are puppets of the United States and U.S. oil companies; this is why they hate us so much.

The Saudi Royal family was given its power to control Arabia, with the help of, first, the British military, and later the American, in return for exclusive oil concessions. A Bush company subsidiary, Vinnel, provides the private army to protect the House of Saud, because the royal family is hated by their people. Saudi Arabia is a dictatorship, as most oil-producing nations are, and their people would like a democracy, and to see their vast oil wealth used to develop their country so they can all prosper. That's why Arabs are willing to blow themselves up. We keep these royal families in power in exchange for the rights to their oil. The whole Middle East is controlled by the oil conglomerates that put in place leaders who will give them oil concessions, while the United States military exercises its muscle to keep them in power and keep competing oil companies out. This is why there is so much anger toward America and the oil companies in the Middle East: they all know their leaders are puppets and America and the oil giants control their countries, while Americans are unaware and unconcerned, as long as the oil keeps flowing. Their acts of terror, as wrong as they are, are the direct result of our own acts of terror on them.

According to the National Security Council, America's support for Israel is explicitly to maintain a regional presence and maintain power over the oil producing nations. We have a whole new army in the Middle East, CenCom, to protect the oil; another Army is being planned to protect the newly found oil resources in Africa, called AfriCom. The Chinese are moving in, we have to keep them in check. It's all about the oil.

Recent Coups for Oil

In 2001, in response to 9/11, U.S. forces invaded Afghanistan to quell the Taliban presence; the very same Taliban created and supported by the United States CIA during the Carter Administration. Upon taking control of the capital, Kabul, the United States installed Hamid Karzai as, first, head of the Afghan Interim Authority and then in 2002 as its president. Before becoming president, Karzai was a top adviser to the UNOCAL oil company, and his first act as president was to approve construction of the Central Asia Gas (CentGas) pipeline that will run from oil rich Turkmenistan through western Afghanistan to Pakistan (the nearest port). Our three main military bases in Afghanistan are spread out along this pipeline. Moreover, according to an article in the *New York Times* by Mark Mazzetti and James Risen, Hamid Karzai's brother, Ahmed Wali Karzai, is one of Afghanistan's largest opium growers and exporters and is supported by the CIA.

Recently, vast oil reserves were discovered near Mogadishu in Somalia. U.S. troops (or freedom fighters) were sent in to help the poor Somalis, but they only freed the area around the new oil fields and the area the pipeline will take the oil to the port in Mogadishu. The warring clans around the rest of the country were left alone. Once the oil was secured our troops went home. In 2007, the Iraq Oil Law (Iraq Hydrocarbon Law) was proposed to the Iraqi Council of Representatives, which receives millions from the United States for serving United States interests. In June of 2008, the Iraqi Oil Ministry announced plans to go along with the proposal that gives Exxon/Mobil and Chevron (all Rockefeller) and some Shell/BP (British Queen own 40 percent of Shell and most of BP) exclusive rights to develop all of Iraq's largest fields. Thus American and British military and political forces have taken control of Iraq's oil. American and British oil companies call the shots.

During the presidential election between John McCain and Barak Obama, a breaking news headline read: "Fighting broke out in the former Soviet satellite state, and now independent democracy, of Georgia." President Bush and Secretary of State Rice claim that the Russians are interfering in Georgia's democracy on the news. Here's what the network news, or the president, isn't going to tell you (John McCain broke the news): First, Georgia lies south of Russia, north of Turkey, on the eastern most edge of the Black Sea, and, more importantly, west of Azerbaijan, one of the largest oil-producing countries in the world. The second largest oil pipeline in the world now runs from Azerbaijan through Georgia to the Black Sea ports. That pipeline was paid for with American taxpayer money through loan guarantees from the Export-Import Bank and the Overseas Private Investment Corporation, a.k.a. the World Bank. In other words, our tax dollars subsidized the pipeline. Azerbaijan used to be controlled by the Soviet Union, and now it is controlled by the American oil giants, primarily Chevron and Conoco-Phillips.

The United States has begun to gain control of the oil in Azerbaijan to the objection of the Russians; it's an economic war. Tim Cejka, president of Exxon Mobil Corporation became the chairman of the U.S. Azerbaijan Chamber of Commerce, and American interests now control the pipeline. We took control away from the Russians. According to the English version of Moscow's news, the Americans are meddling in the Russian oil business and as a retaliatory strike fired missiles at the Georgian pipeline to shut off the supply of oil. According to Russia, it's about the oil. It is important to note that this information is not appearing on our news. The Russians are trying to exert control over the oil, and the United States is making it clear that the oil belongs to U.S. companies now, but the news doesn't make that clear.

We are currently building a large permanent military presence in Iraq, as well as a navy base in Bahrain and other places classified in former soviet states with oil and in North Africa; our military presence must be large enough to keep competing nations from threatening our access the oil. This may be deemed necessary by the government, but the public should be informed, even educated, on the subject so we as a people can make informed decisions. It should not be known to just a few who work secretly and all too often quite self-servingly.

The Executive Branch of Oil

A leading player in the oil game in Iraq is Halliburton. Halliburton not only has the bulk of contracts for Iraq's oil transportation and oil development services, but it is also now our nation's largest defense contractor, providing the food, housing, and other services for our military deployed overseas. Before becoming vice present for George W. Bush, Dick Cheney served as Halliburton's CEO, and before that he served as secretary of defense—the classic revolving door. Cheney's connections with leading government officials helped build Halliburton to its current status as the number-one contractor with the military.

By law, all defense contacts must be subject to competitive bidding, but President Bush used "executive privilege" to usurp this law, and hired Cheney's company. Cheney has publically stated on three occasions on national television that he no longer receives compensation from Halliburton. On all three occasions he has had to retract those statements when it was discovered that, in fact, he has, and still does receive compensation, which is a clear conflict of interest. In 2001 he received $205,298, and in 2002 he received $162,392. He also holds 433,333 unexercised stock options that are becoming increasingly more valuable; not to mention dozens of offshore companies holding undisclosed assets and ownership.

Cheney and Halliburton were indicted and under federal investigation with the Justice Department (in two separate investigations), but when President Bush was elected president he had the Justice Department drop the charges claiming "executive privilege." Most of the real money in these contacts is held in holding companies and trusts in offshore accounts, such as, the Cayman Islands. The reasons for this are to conceal the ownership and interests of the principals and to "protect" their assets, or defer them, from taxation. Before Cheney became CEO of Halliburton, it had nine offshore companies; during Cheney's reign they created fifty-eight (or more). Tens of billions of dollars are reportedly held in those offshore accounts.

Halliburton now has the largest exclusive military contact in history and a virtual monopoly on both servicing U.S. troops deployed overseas (what is called LOGCAP) and in servicing the oil production in Iraq. The Bush-Halliburton relationship goes back quite a bit too: George H. W. Bush (Sr.) used to work for Dresser Industries, which was a subdivision of Halliburton. Most of Halliburton's key executives and board members are ex-government officials, high-ranking military officers, and leadership in the Department of Defense, who are given lucrative consulting contacts after retiring from government service. These same employees become the lobbyists for Halliburton and secure the government contacts that make them so much money.

The other significant conflict of interest is with the Bush's and the Carlyle Group, which was one of the largest investors in defense contacting and holding companies in the world, although it had recently diversified after receiving public exposure. George Bush (Sr.) is both a major stockholder and consultant for them, traveling the globe bringing defense contracts to them. George Bush (Jr.) used to work for a division of Carlyle called CraterAir back in 1993 (a point not on his official resume). Both Bush's are owners in the company, as are the Saudi Royal family and Bin Laden family as well as many other top military brass and former Department of Defense leaders. Carlyle is a holding company that invests in the stock of other companies and plays a key role in military contracting.

One of Carlyle's holdings, Braddock, Dunn, McDonald, or BDM, is one of the leading defense consulting companies in the world (a division of Ford Aerospace). BDM has won what is called a "basic ordering agreement," which is an open-ended, ongoing, long-term contact with the Pentagon. They help decide which military and defense contacts the Pentagon should accept, and do the background checks on all high ranking military or government employees. You have to go through them to be well placed in any government position; they can make you or break you.

Another of Carlyle's holding is Vinnell, which hires ex-special forces personnel, and maintains one of the largest private armies in the world. These mercenaries and are used to help protect the Saudi Royal Family and perform actions that the U.S. government can deny involvement with, including assassinations... On the board of the Carlyle Group is Frank Carlucci, former secretary of defense and deputy director of the CIA, and James Baker III, former secretary of state under George Bush Sr., Richard Dorman, former director of the office of management and budget also under George Bush Sr., and Colin Powell, former chief of staff of the military and secretary of state for George Bush Jr., as well as, John Major, former prime minister of the United Kingdom and many prominent British statesmen.

The World's Oil

From the supply side, there are two key figures to consider when looking at global oil, one is oil production and the other is proven oil reserves, on the demand side it's important to look at refining capacity and demand. Oil production refers to the barrels of crude oil extracted each day from drilling operations. This should not be confused with oil supply, which refers to market availability that might include natural gas, bioethanol or other sources (Source: CIA World Fact book):

World Oil Production

Rank	Country	Production (bbl/day)	Date
1	Russia	9,920,000	2009
2	Saudi Arabia	8,146,000	2008
3	United States	4,950,000	2008
4	Iran	4,127,000	2009
5	China	3,991,000	2009
6	Canada	3,220,000	2008
7	Mexico	2,602,000	2009
-	European	2,531,000	2007
8	Iraq	2,420,000	2009
9	Norway	2,380,000	2008
10	UAE	2,271,000	2008

The Arab League produces 26,419,000 bbl/day (2008), and World production is 85,160,000 bbl/day (2008); that's 31 percent. Kuwait comes in at number eleven in production. The whole country is essentially one big oil field, with 2,271,000 bbl/day (2008).

Most industry analysts believe we have reached **Peak Oil**, which means even as demand is rising at an increasing rate, the amount of oil we can extract is diminishing; thus industrial nations around the world are vying to control the world oil supply. Tar sands, deeper wells, and more remote locations also provide future oil reserves but at much greater cost.

Proven oil reserves are compiled by the industry and the CIA, but most oil companies don't show all their data. What figures we have for global reserves for 2010 from *The World Factbook* are as follows:

Rank	Country	Reserves (bbl)	Market
1	Saudi Arabia	264,100,000,000	19.78%
2	Canada	178,100,000,000	13.21%
3	Iran	150,310,000,000	11.10%
4	Iraq	143,100,000,000	10.60%
5	Kuwait	101,500,000,000	8.71%
6	Venezuela	98,590,000,000	7.37%
7	UAE	97,800,000,000	7.25%
8	Russia	79,800,000,000	4.45%
9	Libya	46,000,000,000	3.24%
10	Nigeria	36,220,000,000	2.69%
11	Kazakhstan	30,000,000,000	2.22%
12	Qatar	27,190,000,000	1.13%
13	United States	21,320,000,000	1.58%
14	China	15,700,000,000	1.19
15	Algeria	15,150,000,000	.90%

Followed by Angola, Mexico, Brazil, Azerbaijan, Sudan, Norway, India, European Union, Oman, and Vietnam. Vietnam just borrowed $1 billion to finance the Dung Quat oil refinery, partnering with ConocoPhillips and obtaining financing through BNP Paribas, and they are now expected to become a regional leader. Vietnam has large oil reserves, but that was only made public after the Vietnam War. PetroVietnam is carrying out exploration activities in Malaysia, Indonesia, Mongolia, and Algeria. But the center of oil is the Middle East.

If you add the Middle Eastern states of Saudi Arabia, Iran, Iraq, Kuwait, United Arab Emirates (UAE), and Qatar, that amounts to **58.57 percent of the known oil reserves in the world**. Much of Canada's reserves are in tars and sands that are difficult and expensive to extract and the United States just can't produce as much oil as it needs, this places critical importance on foreign oil in the Middle East.

The Geo-Politics of Oil

The vast majority of the world's oil reserves are in Islamic countries. Islam recognizes the same biblical God as the Jews and Christians—El, Al or Yah—Muslims call God by the Arabic name Allah, Al-lah, the God. They recognize the prophets of the Jews, see Jesus as a prophet of God as the early Semitic Christians did, and write more about the Holy Mother Mary (mother of Jesus) than is written in the Holy Bible. However, they also believe that God chose another prophet, Mohammad, and his revelation is the Koran the holy scripture of Islam. Islam is now overtaking Christianity as the world's largest religion, and is primarily predominant in the Middle East, North Africa to the equator, India to Central Asia, and the southern states of the former Soviet Union. Islam is comprised of two predominate groups: the Sunni, the majority and host to Islam's most holy cities of Mecca and Medina in Saudi Arabia.

The other major sect is called Shia, and it is primarily active within the former Persian Empire, mostly Iran, southern Iraq, and Yemen.

There is a deep resentment within the Muslim community toward the United States, due in part to its support of Israel, as well as for supporting dictators in their countries and taking their oil. Westerners tend to think we are liberating and modernizing third world countries, which in many cases we may be, but within Islam they see our presence in their countries as another Crusade, a conquest and subjugation of their people for oil. Only the very few get rich in those countries, and most of the people are poor and can't even vote. In Saudi Arabia and other Sunni countries, Shia are not allowed to hold public office, become judges, or serve as witnesses in court; this has created resentment between the two sects.

Iran is a Shia nation and so is Yemen; both have oil and both sit on the two greatest flows of oil in the world. Most of the world's oil moves through the Strait of Hormuz in the Persian Gulf, and Iran hugs this little straight geographically like a bear holding a cub; at its narrowest chock point it's only thirty miles across, and an average of fifteen tankers pass through it each day.

Yemen, another Shia state, lies upon the Gate of Tears, another narrow straight near the southern Saudi oil fields, through which 3.3 million barrels of oil are shipped every day. Yemenis' and Saudis have been fighting border battles, and Saudi Arabia was accused of giving Saddam's Iraq billions of dollars, with the help of the United States, to kill Shia in Iran. A half a million Iranians died, and they feel the other oil countries were merely puppets of the United States, so the Shia are mobilizing for war. The people of Iran also had their democratically elected leader overthrown with the help of the United States, so they fear we will try to take over their country again to steal their oil. This is the underpinning of global terrorism. When you look at the true cost of oil, including our massive military and aid expenditures, the price at the pump would be more than double. We spend a fortune for cheap oil, and it costs lives, and now most of the world hates the West. We are creating a breeding ground for more war.

The world's oldest oil fields in Baku, Texas, and Venezuela have dried up. Production is slowing down in most of the oil producing nations. Saudi Arabia and Iraq show the best future prospects and they are both highly volatile nations. The standard of living for the average Saudi Arabian is half what it used to be and they don't have much of a future, so they are turning to religion for comfort and direction. They are also resenting the west for dominating their land again.

In every Islamic oil-producing nation these anti-West sentiments are building. The view is that big American oil companies make deals with people they put into power, and/or protect with their military might, and the few get astoundingly rich and while most of the rest have very little, and they suffer. The images on the television they watch are of Americans controlling everything, and they have a point, we do. If these nations rose up together they could cripple the oil infrastructure and it would hit the west hard, so U.S. military bases are going up everywhere there is oil. The oil must flow.

Moreover, the images on television that most of the world sees shows the United States as a world of wealth and comfort they can only dream of; they also see the lowest common denominator of social behavior, and what appears to them as immoral behavior and lascivious conduct, as well as the mind-boggling technology and military power that is both awesome and intimidating. Wherever the Westerner goes, he brings alcohol, drugs, debt, and war, so over the past few decades the world both looks up to America but also is scared of it. We get rich off of other peoples resources, and more of the world is getting wiser to it. Without tending to the needs and rights of the common man, the laborers, we lead ourselves to more rebellions and wars.

Project for the New American Century

In 1997 the Project for the New American Century (PNAC) was created as an educational organization whose goal is to promote American global leadership. The original signatories include Dick Cheney, Jeb Bush, Elliott Abrams, Dan Quayle, Donald Rumsfeld, and Paul Wolfowitz, and others from presidential cabinets, defense contractors, and universities. The PNAC's policy document *Rebuilding America's Defenses: Strategy, Forces, and Resources for a New Century* describes its mission in the introduction:

> In broad terms, we saw the project as building upon the defense strategy outlined by the Cheney Defense Department in the waning days of the Bush Administration. The Defense Policy Guidance (DPG) drafted in the early months of 1992 provided a blueprint for maintaining U.S. preeminence, precluding the rise of a great power rival, and shaping the international security order in line with American principles and interests.

This policy document has served as the bases of military actions since its creation, it declares, "America's grand strategy should aim to preserve and extend this advantageous position as far into the future as possible." Its four core missions for U.S. military forces include:

Defend the American homeland

Fight and decisively win multiple, simultaneous major theater wars

Perform the "constabulary" duties associated with shaping the security environment in critical regions.

Transform U.S. forces to exploit the "revolution in military affairs."

This document further suggests in which area of defense American should invest, which include Modernize the F-22 fighter, expand submarine and surface combatant fleets; expand and deploy global missile defenses and modernize our nuclear capabilities; "pave the way" for both space and "cyberspace" military forces; develop greater military technology; increase defense spending; and enlarge the size of our military personnel, and consider a draft. The most controversial statement of the report in section V of Rebuilding America's Defenses, entitled "Creating Tomorrow's Dominant Force," and it includes the sentence: "Further, the process of transformation, even if it brings revolutionary change, is likely to be a long one, absent some catastrophic and catalyzing event like a new Pearl Harbor." Something like 9/11.

Energy

Total worldwide energy consumption in 2008 was 474 exajoules, with almost 90 percent derived from the combustion of fossil fuels like oil; this is equivalent to an overall average power consumption rate of fifteen terawatts. One terawatt is equal to one trillion watts (a typical lighting strike); a typical household incandescent lightbulb has a power rating of 25 to 100 watts, and a typical coal-powered power station produces around 600-700 megawatts. A megawatt is one million watts. Of all the energy harnessed since the industrial revolution, more than half has been consumed within the last two decades, this is primarily due to the rise of a middle class and increasing global population. China became the world's largest energy consumer, 18 percent of total, when its consumption surged from 4 percent in 2008 to 8 percent in 2009, the United States is the world's second largest consumer of energy, but it's consumption is down slightly due to the economic recession (2011).

Oil still remains the largest energy source, 33 percent, despite the fact that its share has been decreasing over time. Coal still plays an important role of feeding the world's energy consumption accounting for 27 percent in 2009, followed by gas 23 percent (2005), Nuclear 6 percent (2005), Biomass 4 percent (2005), Hydro 3 percent (2005), Solar 0.5 percent (2005) and wind 0.3 percent. Most of the world's energy comes from the sun, and in the past few decades science has made tremendous strides of harnessing the sun's energy, of particular importance is making this technology commercially available in building materials and using it in structures. This technology already exists and prototypes are in use today; we have only to mobilize the resources such as capital to bring it into production.

The technology also exists today to manufacture energy from the wind at commercially competitive prices, and within two decades we could supply enough electricity to support North America's needs, including the anticipated increase in electric cars. At the end of 2009, worldwide wind farm capacity increased 31 percent to 157,900 MW. Wind now supplies 1.3 percent of global electricity production: 19 percent in Denmark, 9 percent in Spain and Portugal, and 6 percent in Germany and Ireland. In 2008, United States wind power capacity reached 25,170 MW and is expected to increase at an increasing rate. However, even with massive infrastructure development in wind and solar, we are still going to need more fossil fuels in the foreseeable future. Moreover, oil is also used in other industries such as plastics and fertilizers, so the oil needs to keep coming even as we develop more sensible renewable energy sources.

The Enron Loophole

Enron serves as a classic example of what's wrong with business and government. Here is an example of how a lobbyist can buy influence and power all the way up to the president. In some countries, energy is managed as a public service; however, in the United States and many other countries it is a commodity traded on the market. As a market commodity it not only is heavily influenced by market conditions but also by those who would manipulate the market for personal gain at the expense of others.

Enron Corporation became traders of energy and controlled much of the market. Texas Senator Phil Gramm, one of the all-time top financial recipients of the oil and gas industry, led the pack for Enron to get a loophole in regulation that would enable Enron to manipulate the energy market. Enron's CEO Ken Lay served as the regional chairman of Gramm's unsuccessful campaign for the Republican presidential election. Senator Gramm's wife, Wendy Gramm, served on Enron's board from 1993 to 2002, made millions, and served on the auditing committee responsible for Enron's financial reporting. In her book *The Tyranny of Oil*, Antonia Juhasz, reveals that "Both the company and its top officers were George W. Bush's single greatest career campaign contributor."

In December of 2000, without any congressional hearings or debate, Phil Gramm was able to add what has been labeled the "Enron Loophole" into the **Commodity Futures Modernization Act**. This bill was quickly attached to a 11,000-page omnibus appropriations bill and signed into law. They slipped it in. This enabled the traders to create an unregulated exchange and take control of the energy market; this is what ultimately led to the energy crisis and rolling blackouts in California. Enron stuck it to California and made a financial killing. This act also enabled the energy industry to form a new syndicate called the InterContinental Exchange (ICE) to create an unregulated energy futures market. ICE was founded by BP, Shell, TotalFinaElf, Goldman Sachs, Morgan Stanley, and others, and uses many of the same traders who took Enron down. Traders openly admitted manipulating the markets and that was, in fact, their job, stating explicitly in hearings: "Yes, we moved markets." In 1999 California paid $7.4 billion for wholesale electricity, and only one year later the cost rose 277 percent to $27.1 billion.

According to Michael Greenberger in the 2007 Senate hearings stated:

> It is now beyond doubt that manipulation of futures and derivatives contracts pursuant to that loophole dramatically increased the market price of electricity in the Western United States during 2001-2002.

Another typical example of how corporations have been mismanaged, the same company that is giving Enron advice on how to hide assets and liabilities in offshore accounts so the stockholders, the public and the government can't see it, Arthur Anderson, a leading public accountancy corporation at the time, was also retained by Enron to audit the company on behalf of the stockholders. This is obviously a conflict of interest, and Arthur Anderson ultimately went under for it; but these same practices still go on to this day.

Hiding money in offshore accounts, lying to stockholders, manipulating markets, and paying off politicians to get loopholes or kickbacks and subsidies, this is at the heart of what's hurting the people of the world; unrestrained lobbying is corrupting our nation, and it goes all the way to the top. The United States Congress has sold out to corporate interests, but they can't survive in the system we have now otherwise. We have to change the system, and we have to kill lobbying.

Cartel Lobby Power

Most states and countries receive a tax for the extraction of their natural resources, in order to help support the infrastructure they use and give something back to the communities that have these resources. California is home to some of the nation's largest oil companies, such as Chevron, but many oil companies drill up and down the coast. Almost all state and national representatives receive money from the oil syndicate, so moving any legislation that the oil companies don't want is going to be very difficult.

In 2006 voters added **Proposition 87** on the ballet in order to tax that oil that California owned and was being drawn out and sold for profit by the oil companies. It was a relatively small tax compared to what other states imposed. Before the ballet was placed to a vote, polls suggested over 60 percent of the voters were in favor of the idea. However, when the measure was coming up for the California voters the oil companies poured over $100 million dollars through their network to convince the voter it would just end up costing them more at the pumps, which wouldn't necessarily have to be true, only if the board decided to. The voters were scared and voted against taxing the oil companies. Those proposing the tax were simply outspent.

The oil interests outspend the voters' interests two to one. This is a basic formula many political and special interests have learned that winning is very much based on how much airtime you have. The more money you have, the more airtime you can buy; the more airtime you have the greater your chances of winning. So the corporate strategy is to outspend your opponent for ads, lobbying, lawsuits, and buying support from constituents. The Center for Responsive Politics (CRP), using the **Federal Election Commission** data estimates that from 1998-2006 ExxonMobil alone spent more than $80 million lobbying the federal government. Chevon spent over $50 million. The price of winning an election has gone up to $9.6 million for a senate seat and $1.25 million for a seat in the House of Representatives; the oil industry spent over $240 million lobbying the government and got their mergers. These figures do not even include the "soft money" that goes to conventions, parties, and affiliations that support a candidate, and this soft money is many times larger than direct reported lobbying. Almost every United States senator, representative, and president is beholding to the oil monopoly and the banking cartel, which are the same interests.

Anyone goes against the will of this oil cartel finds a fortune will be spent on any opposing candidate in the next election. The entire government of the United States is paid off and beholding to these special interests. The Sherman Antitrust Act, the most famous antitrust act in United States history, was recently overturned allowing all the former Standard Oil giants to merge together again. Shortly thereafter the price of oil reached record heights at the pumps the same time they were recording world record profits. Moreover, our Supreme Court just overruled two important precedents about the First Amendment rights of corporations in 2010 and ruled that government may not ban political spending by corporations in candidate elections. President Barak Obama called it:

> [A] major victory for big oil, Wall Street banks, health insurance companies, and the other powerful interests that marshal their power every day in Washington to drown out the voices of everyday Americans.

So, now, if you have enough money you can buy all the candidates or votes that you want, and that is at the heart of our democracies failings. Our congressmen do the bidding of those who put them in power, and the power is with the money. The biggest money interests are corporations. In an interview with Marcia Coyle of the *National Law Journal* explaining the Supreme Court's radical departure from its own legal precedents on *PBS Newsline* explaining that the political influence on the Supreme Court have "swung from deference to congressional regulation to, basically, deregulation." Moreover, many of the corporations that are sponsoring our representatives are heavily owned by foreigners who don't necessarily have the best interests of the United States at heart. Furthermore, much of the lobbying that goes on is in secret, and money is transferred and held in secret offshore accounts, in places like the Cayman Islands. **The Center for Public Integrity** goes even further to say:

> What is not well understood by the American People is the substantially lawless extent to which the political parties launder hundreds of millions of dollars throughout [these committees].

Offshore banks and corporations are used by the rich to hind assets or avoid (defer) paying taxes. Most really wealthy people don't pay taxes. Countries that offer lower or no taxes include the Channel Islands "offshore" of Great Britain (Isle of Man and Guernsey), or little countries like Switzerland, Luxembourg, and Andorra as well as various island nations in the Caribbean like the Cayman islands.

Tax Justice Network estimates that global tax revenue lost to tax havens exceeds $225 billion a year. Estimates by the Organization for Economic Cooperation and Development (OECD) estimates that by 2007 capital held offshore amounts to somewhere between $5 trillion and $7 trillion, making up approximately 6-8 percent of total global investments under management; over $1 trillion is held in the Cayman Islands alone.

Approximately one-third of all corporate revenue flows through offshore entities, and corporations avoid paying taxes on that revenue. Taxes on those revenues could make a substantial contribution to our economy, but special laws allow them to cheat the American taxpayer who carries the tax burden. Moreover, during this same period ExxonMobil received more than $4 billion in tax breaks, Conoco Philips received $2 billion in tax breaks. Corporations are required to pay a 35 percent effective tax rate, most pay less than half or none at all. Americans are none the wiser; the Congress is run by corporations, and the Supreme Court no longer protects the American people.

World Bank Group

The World Bank group is the result of the Bretton Woods agreement of 1945, and comprises of five international organizations that, together, make leveraged loans to other countries to support their development. These five groups are:

International Bank for Reconstruction and Development (IBRD)

International Development Association (IDA)

International Finance Corporation (IFC)

Multilateral Investment Guarantee Agency (MIGA)

International Centre for Settlement of Investment Disputes (ICSID)

The IBRD and IDA provide loans to member countries and make grants to very poor countries. Loans or grants for specific projects are often linked to wider policy changes in certain sectors or in the economy. The IFC and MIGA make investments into the private sector and provide insurance respectively. The World Bank is part of the United Nations system, but the major contributor is the United States, thus, the president of the United States nominates the president of the World Bank and elected by the Federal Reserve Board Bank's Board of Governors. Most of the leadership is drawn from the Federal Reserve. Moreover, three former Chase Manhattan Bank presidents—John J. McCloy, Eugene R. Black, Sr., and George Woods—all led the World Bank as president, and a fourth, James D. Wolfensohn, served as director of the Rockefeller Foundation. Rockefeller served as chairman of the Chase Manhattan bank for years, and meetings of the World Bank and International Monetary fund are often funded by the Rockefellers.

The International Monetary Fund or IMF

The World Bank Group works in conjunction with the International Monetary Fund, the Federal Reserve and other commercial banks to manage world economics. The IMF is a global financial system that oversees the macroeconomic policies of its member countries. Policy management includes stabilization of currency exchange rates and balance of payments.

The IMF also creates a form of money they call **Special Drawing Rights** or SDRs, which are considered international foreign exchange reserve assets, representing a claim to foreign currencies that can be exchanged for currencies in time of need; it creates more money to lend to countries and institutions. Conditions for loans typically involve structural adjustment programs that typically include privatization of natural resources, deregulation, and removal of trade barriers. Countries that fail to enact these programs are often subject to severe fiscal discipline. Foreign nations benefit from the capital creation that can be used to fund infrastructure and commercial, agricultural, and industrial development, but often become debt encumbered and lose control over their natural resources.

The World Bank Group and IMF, working with multinational banks and corporations, have done an amazing job at helping developing countries develop infrastructure, industry, mining and increased the standard of living in many countries; however, many countries complain how they become deeply in debt and end up losing control of their economy and political power always goes to those who secure economic interests. One former international economist, writer for the *Economist* magazine and best-selling author of *Confessions of an Economic Hit Man,* John Perkins, says developing nations are neutralized politically, their wealth gaps driven wider, and economies crippled in the long run. Perkins, now retired and guilty, describes his role, and that of others in the industry, as being economic hit men, a role he describes as follows:

> Economic hit men are highly paid professionals who cheat countries around the globe out of trillions of dollars. They funnel money from the World Bank, the U.S. Agency for International Development, and other foreign "aid" organizations into the coffers of huge corporations and the pockets of a few wealthy families who control the planet's natural resources. Their tools included fraudulent financial reports, rigged elections, payoffs, extortion, sex, and murder. They play a game as old as empire, but one that has taken on new and terrifying dimensions during this time of globalization.

An example of how some countries feel manipulated by the Cartel, there is an offer by the **G8** nations to forgive Third World debt, but it is conditioned on the privatization of their health, education, electric, water, and other public services, as well as the removal any trade barriers on imports, taxes, and tariffs. The World Bank Group and IMF are currently working on developing a world currency and a system in which all the banks go through one central bank. This new globally centralized banking scheme has been gaining strength, and in 2002 at the **London Global Summit** it was announced:

> We have also agreed today additional resources of one trillion dollars that are available to the world economy through the International Monetary Fund and other institutions. This includes 250 billion in Special Drawing Rights of the reserve currency of the IMF—A New World Order is emerging.

National Debt

The current gross federal debt as a percentage of GDP, as of the end of 2009, was **83.4 percent**. Our current national debt is the highest it has been since the late 1940s, where the deficit was over 100 percent at the end of World War II. The president proposes a budget for the government to the congress, which can amend it before passing. The gross federal debt has become one of the most important figures in evaluating the strength of the United States economy.

The following graph lists the growth in our debt relative to our gross domestic product (how much we owe relative to how much we make) and the increase and decrease in debt spending per administration. After World War II our debt increased but decreased as a percent of our GDP, but after President Nixon dropped the Bretton Woods agreement, took us off the gold standard, and began deficit spending as part of the cold war arms race, our debt began to rise (Debt/GDP as of the start of the presidential administration):

United States National Debt

President	Term	Debt/GDP
Nixon/Ford	1973-1977	35.6%/0.2%
Jimmy Carter	1977-1981	35.2%/-3.3%
Ronald Reagan	1981-1985	32.5%/11.3%
Ronald Reagan	1985-1989	43.8%/9.3%
George H.W. Bush	1989-1993	51.1%/15.0%
Bill Clinton	1993-1997	66.1%/-0.7%
Bill Clinton	1997-2001	65.4%/-0.9%
George Bush	2001-2005	56.4%/7.1%
George Bush	2005-2009	63.4%/20.0%
Barack Obama	2009-	83.4%

Most countries are heavily indebted; as of December 2009 the world was $56,900,000,000,000 in external debt. External debt is the total public and private debt owed to nonresidents repayable in foreign currency, goods or services, where public debt is the money owed by the government to a central bank or banking group (source: Wikipedia 2009).

International Debt

Country	External Debt ($)	Per capita	% GDP
United States	$13,450,000,000,000	$43,758	94%
UK	9,088,000,000,000	$147,060	415%
Germany	5,208,000,000,000	$63,493	155%
France	5,021,000,000,000	$80,209	188%

Netherlands	3,733,000,000,000	$226,503	470%
Spain	2,410,000,000,000	$52,588	165%
Italy	2,328,000,000,000	$39,234	101%
Ireland	2,287,000,000,000	$515,671	1004%
Japan	2,132,000,000,000	$16,714	42%

The other European countries are also heavily in debt; Russia's per capita debt is only $2,611 and the percentage of GDP is 7 percent; the People's Republic of China per capita debt is only $260 and only 7 Percent of their GDP. Almost every country in the world is deeply in debt to both the World Banking Group and commercial banks, which also make loans to other countries, directly or through their national banks. Ultimately, every country in the world is beholding to the world-banking cartel.

Gross Domestic Production

Gross Domestic Production (GDP) measures the amount of goods and services exchanged in a year; it indicates the overall size of a nation's economy. In president Barak Obama's State of the Union Address, January 2011, he provided an overview of the world's largest economies:

United States	$14.0 Trillion
China	$5.7 Trillion
Japan	$5.3 Trillion
Germany	$3.3 Trillion
France	$2.5 Trillion

The United States economy is greater in size than the next three largest economies (China, Japan, and Germany) combined.

The real median household income in America was $52,301 in 2000, and in 2009 it dropped to $49,777; that's a decline of $2,524 according to the president's statistics. As the money supply has decreased, but more importantly credit has been severely restricted, our money inflated, and commerce and employment diminished.

Economic Indicators

In the United States the inflation rate in consumer prices was 2.782 percent in 2009 and 1.395 percent in 2010, which is low considering we are in a recession. The unemployment rate in the United States is around 9 percent as of January 2011, that's about twice as high as is normal.

China's unemployment rate is 4.1 percent, Japan's 5.1 percent, the European Union as a whole is 9.7 percent, and most of the rest of the world is much higher. According to the U.S. Bureau of Labor Statistics in their Ten Year Occupational Employment Projections, over the 2008-2018 decade, total employment is projected to increase by 15.3 million jobs, or 10 percent. That's up from 10.4 million jobs in the preceding decade. According the U.S. Bureau of Labor Statistics, productivity rose 2.6 percent in the nonfarm business sector in the fourth quarter of 2010; unit labor costs declined 0.6 percent; annual average productivity increased 3.6 percent from 2009 to 2010.

In 2008, multifactor productivity decreased at a 0.7 annual rate in the manufacturing sector, grew 0.3 percent in durable manufacturing, and fell 1.6 percent in nondurable manufacturing. In Gross Domestic Production (GDP) per capita, which measures a nation's productivity, the United States ranks third behind Norway and Singapore, and ahead of Ireland, Netherlands, Australia, Austria, Canada, Sweden, Denmark, the United Kingdom, Germany, Belgium, Finland, France, Spain, Japan, Italy, and Korea.

The Money Supply

The money supply is the total amount of money available in an economy at any particular point in time. The measurement of M1 includes all notes and coin in circulation and checks, M2 includes savings accounts, and M3 adds funds in time deposits and money market accounts. As of November 2009 the Federal Reserve reported that the U.S. dollar monetary base is $1,999,897,000,000, an increase of 142 percent in two years. M2 has increased from $7.41 trillion in 2007 to $8.36 in 2009, an increase of 12.9 percent.

A few years ago the Federal Reserve stopped publishing the figures for **M3**, but this indicator more accurately reflects the creation of new money and credit as M3 includes the large institutional investments. In addition to shrinking the money supply, the Federal Reserve and commercial banking system can simply restrict the amount of loans they make. This lack of available funds is what has put the brakes on the economy.

Too little credit hurts us, and too much credit isn't good either; the supply of money and credit needs to be balanced with the needs of the community and nation. Extending too much credit or making money too available inflates the currency, and leads to bad investments. Non-debt-based funds are needed to spur economic growth without inflating the currency; commodity based or asset based currency is always stronger than fiat money and debt based currency.

Consumer Credit

Consumer credit includes credit cards, store cards, automobile finance, personal loans, retail installment loans, and home mortgages. Interest on borrowed money is reflected in an annual percentage rate (APR), which is designed to reflect the total costs to the borrower, including fees not reflected in the rate of interest alone.

Credit risk is typically scored by independent firms, the largest in the United States being Experian, Equifax, and Trans Union. Dun & Bradstreet is the nation's commercial-credit reporting company. Types of credit include: cash credit, working capital, bank overdraft, term loan, bill discounting, project financing and letters of credit, which are typically securitized or collateralized with some assets or promises.

Debt

In 2004 worldwide debt and equity underwriting reached a record $5.69 trillion; while world debt underwriting grew to $5.19 trillion (Thomson Financial data). In the same year syndicated lending climbed to over $163 billion, and asset-backed securities $857 billion. As of 2009, the size of the worldwide bond market (total debt outstanding) was estimated at $82.2 trillion, and the size of the outstanding U.S. bond debt was $31.2 trillion (according to BIS). In 2006 total bond fund net inflows increased to $60.8 billion.

Financial Position of the United States - 2008/Q1

Credit market debt	$49.6 trillion	349 percent (GDP)
Household sector	$13,959.9 billion	99 percent
Domestic financial	$15.9 trillion	112 percent

| Nonfinancial corp. | $6.474 trillion | 46 percent |
| Government | $5.22 trillion | |

According to the Federal Reserves Consumer Credit statistical release, dated January 7, 2011, revolving credit decreased again at an annual rate of 6.25 percent and nonrevolving credit increased at an annual rate of 4.24 percent. In 2009 total revolving credit was $865.8 billion and Nonrevolving $1583.5 billion.

The ratio of household debt to disposable personal income is called the **Consumer Leverage Ratio**; and it is used to quantify the amount of debt the average American consumer has, relative to his/her disposable income. The historical average ratio in 1975 has been 0.9x, but the ratio has increased to 1.24x in Q3 2009 (Federal Reserve); this means the average American owes more than he or she makes, and collectively Americans are losing their net worth. Almost everyone owes the bank, and the whole financial industry has control over those who owe. We are enslaved by debt, and the average American never gets out. The whole world is controlled by money and credit, and those who control money and credit control the world, i.e., governments, corporations, and individuals.

Globalization

A century ago corporations were rare, a device for the wealthy. Now, almost everyone in the West works for one, or has one, and we are all dependent on working with them. They are legal entities not people with feelings, and they serve to make the owners money not necessarily to benefit their employees, community or country. Corporations have grown larger than governments, and wield more control over our lives than any president or congressman. Each year more big corporations buy or merge with smaller corporations creating the world's first superconglomerates, the biggest institutions and economic powers the world has ever known.

All large corporations work with corporations from other countries, and each country has its own laws, tariffs, and trade restrictions to protect their citizens from unfair practices or corporate abuses. If corporations can lift restrictions, they can make more money for their stockholders. So the lobbying power of the largest corporate interests all focus on lifting restrictions and creating higher authority and laws for multinational transactions so governments, and national laws, don't get in the way of profits. Having varying tariffs and national laws do complicate things, and trade agreements certainly do have their place, but these new laws often usurp the laws and will of the citizens and have constantly created a negative impact on the economy as a whole, specifically the standard of living for the average man.

The North American Free Trade Agreement (**NAFTA**) and other legislation that opens up all markets, also forces corporations to always buy cheaper abroad if they can. Thus, many jobs have migrated to other countries, and American exports have diminished, as it is often cheaper to purchase goods and services abroad. Business choices are made on whatever is in the stockholders' interest, not the employees or the nation, that's why regulations and governance are needed.

Tariffs can and have been used to support domestic production, but corporate lobbies have pushed hard against this. On the other hand the American taxpayer would be amazed to see the billions of subsidies large profitable corporations get from the government. Lobbyists get paid to pay our representatives money, typically campaign contributions, and in return the corporations get earmarks, rebates, and subsidies from the federal government. Congressmen and senators are routinely paid off.

Creating tariffs or restrictions on imports can also influence other countries to create restrictions and tariffs on U.S. imports. The question is does our government act in the interest of its citizens and their employment and development, or is it based on where the most profit can be made for the corporations? Who really has the ear of our legislators? Protecting and policing trade is not the same as restricting trade; investing in our own economy and offering tax incentives to employ more Americans makes us more competitive.

Mega Mergers

We are in a unique time in world history where corporations are combining to form giant conglomerates, the likes of which the world has never seen. The biggest mergers have occurred in the last few decades in the industries of banking, oil, telecom, pharmaceuticals, retail, transportation, and computers. Virtually all the major industries are controlled by fewer and fewer corporations and CEOs.

The control of all the trade and commerce of the world is being narrowed down to just a small fraternity of corporate elite, with the money cartel leading the pack. We've covered the oil monopoly, but there are several other key industries to watch. The following highlights some of the bigger and more significant mergers of the last decade.

Communications

The biggest merger to date in U.S. history was that of Internet service provider America Online with the media giant Time Warner for a record of $162 billion in 2001. However, by 2002 the company took at $99 billion dollar loss and today the two companies operate as separate entities. Also in 2002, AT&T spun off its broadband unit to Comcast, which created "the nation's largest cable company," valued at around $60 billion, including stock and debt. Comcast now boasts over "6.3 million digital video customers, 3.3 million broadband customers and 1.3 million cable telephony (VoIP) customers" thus making it the market leader.

In 2000 Qwest merged with U.S. West, and in 1999 Bell Atlantic bought GTE to become Verizon after AT&T's buyout of Tele-Communications Inc, and SCB merged with Ameritech. In 2000 Vodafone AirTouch purchased Mannesmann for $202.8 billion. All over the world telecom, Internet, and media companies have been buying each other up and now there are relatively few who control the entire industry.

Now there are essentially three media empires in the United States, and they are all essentially controlled by the same people:

Time Warner

> AOL
>
> Comuserv
>
> Netscape
>
> Mapquest
>
> HBO
>
> Cable
>
> Cinemax
>
> CNN

Walt Disney

Pixar

Miramax

Touchstone

ABC

News Corporation

20th Century Fox

Direct TV

Fox News

National Geographic and their indaphic

This concentration of media ownership means progressively fewer individuals or organizations control and increasingly large share of the mass media; the majority of media in the world is owned by a proportionately small number of conglomerates and corporations or families. This media concentration affects editorial independence, media bias, conflicts of interest, and freedom of the press.

There are three major television networks in the United States: ABC, CBS, and NBC, with Fox, CNN, and BBC gaining ground. American Broadcasting Company (ABC) is now part of Disney; the Columbia Broadcasting System (CBS) is owned by Westinghouse Electric Corporation/Viacom/CBS Corporation; and the National Broadcasting Company (NBC) is owned by NBC Universal, a joint venture between Comcast and General Electric. Fox Broadcasting Company (FOX) is a part of Rupert Murdoch's News Corporation, and News Corporation is now the world's third-largest media conglomerate behind Disney and Time Warner.

Murdoch was born Australian (now naturalized), and through his FOX media networks he has used the air to call for revolution against a U.S. president. So through corporations foreigners gain control over U.S. interests and minds. Now other countries can influence our media, our politics, or our perceptions. CNN is now owned by Time Warner, too.

There is also an oligopoly in radio ever since the Telecommunications act of 1996, where **Clear Channel Communications** took control of over most of the radio stations round the country (over 1,200 stations). In 2007 the FCC also voted to eliminate the media ownership rules that had been established without debate, including the statute that forbids a single company to own both a newspaper and television or radio station in the same city. Citizens essentially get all their information through the media as its now directed by the heads of just a few corporations that all are part of the same cartel. These conglomerates are owned by the same interests, that is, the same investors. In the last two decades most of the news spend more time with editorials or spinning opinions and less conveying objective facts. It has become infotainment. In an interview in *Fortune* magazine in 2003 Clear Channel chairman Lester Mays clarified his position:

> We're not in the business of providing news and information. We're not in the business of providing well-researched music. We're in the business of selling our customers products.

Not one news source is even giving the public accurate information; much is omitted, most have a strong slant one side or the other and very few people are informed as to what's really going on. Even the tough shows like *Hardball*, *60 minutes*, *Face the Nation*, *Anderson Cooper*, and other's don't really address the most important facts; most of what we get is propaganda that serves political ends. Sponsors affect content, it's about making money and you don't bite the hand that feeds you. The most dangerous aspect of our evolving democracy is that people are losing their ability to think objectively, critically, and independently. Most viewers and listeners are picking sides, their decisions are emotional and directed by others who know how to create "manufactured consent.

Within the **Information Technology** sectors, which include computer software, hardware, and networking infrastructures, the entire industry is again dominated by a few companies. According to the Forbes Global 2000, the major players in this industry are: Apple Inc., IBM, Microsoft, Google (includes YouTube), Accenture, SAP AG, Hewlett Packard, Computer Sciences Corporation, Yahoo, and CA Technologies, and now our largest Internet social networks are owned by these same corporations, all which have common interests. We don't have news not affected by politics or corporate interests.

Lee Atwater, political consultant to Presidents Ronald Reagan and George H.W. Bush and former chairman of the Republican National Committee bragged about leaking over thirty false reports to the press; those reports were routinely used to disseminate false information as the truth. Atwater took credit for spreading the false stories about presidential candidate Walter Mondale that turned the election in Bush Sr.'s favor; Carl Rove has done the same for George W. Bush, and both political parties do it. It's not a matter of blaming a party or an administration, it's an endemic evil within our business culture, and the problem needs attention and oversight. Continually allowing this to occur breeds corporate-government crime, and ultimately hurts the entire economy.

One classic case that demonstrates the dangers of a media monopoly involves Monsanto and **Fox News**, where producers for the channel were doing a story on the Bovine Growth Hormone that is made by Monsanto to cause cows to produce more milk. The reporters found that other countries like Canada were concerned about possible cancer promoting effects on human beings, and the reporters were going to include those studies in their report. After all, it is a public health concern. When Monsanto found out they threatened Fox News with a lawsuit, and the management of Fox News then tried to drop the story, change the story, threatened to fire the reporters if they didn't, and then tried to bribed them to keep it quiet. They were eventually fired and blacklisted. Reporters now know what they can or cannot report.

The television show *60 Minutes* had a similar corporate battle with a story on the Tobacco industry, who threatened to sue *60 Minutes* if they ran the story and remove corporate sponsorship; then they were bought and the holding company put pressure to stop the story. People's lives were threatened. Another producer for *60 Minutes* was scheduled to produce a segment on E. Howard Hunt's confession, that has been recorded, but corporate came down and blocked it. Censorship does exist in the United States, and it needs the public's attention.

These are not isolated examples; the news is controlled by corporations now. It's only getting worse and Americans continue to be in the dark because the news is not going to report it. Anchorman Lou Dobbs spoke out and got bullets shot through his window, and many other reporters have been threatened and it goes unreported out of fear of the government, or cartel, reprisal.

If the citizenry is complicit, then we will continue to have corrupt governments. Our press must be more accountable, and our citizenry better informed. There is an information war going on for our minds and the corporations are winning. Quoting president Thomas Jefferson again:

The only security of all is in a free press. The force of public opinion cannot be resisted when permitted freely to be expressed. The agitation it produces must be submitted to. It is necessary, to keep the waters pure.

Banking

The financial industry is undergoing a major change and one group is rising to the top in dominance. Recently, Bank of New York acquired Mellon; Wachovia acquired World Savings; Bank of America acquired U.S. Trust and then Merrill Lynch; JPMorgan and Chase merged to form JPMorgan Chase and then acquired Bear Stearns and Washington Mutual; Wells Fargo acquired Wachovia, and PNC took National City.

In 1998 Citicorp and Travelers Group merged to form Citigroup, a primary dealer in U.S. Treasury securities and one of the new big four banking conglomerate of: Citigroup, JP Morgan Chase, Bank of America, and Wells Fargo. In 1952 James Stillman Rockefeller was elected president and then chairman in 1959, serving until 1967, and in 1960 his cousin David Rockefeller became president of the Chase Manhattan Bank, now JPMorgan Chase. Moreover, if you look at the institutional holdings of each bank you see they share common interests, interlocking directorates, and they all control the Federal Reserve. Banking is a monopoly with common family interests.

The bailout bill was created by a small group of insiders in the executive branch and the Federal Reserve, and the Congress was, to a large degree, cut out of the decision. The initial bailout bill was not secret and was rejected in Congress, the final version of the bill was kept secret from the Congress until minutes before the vote, so our representatives never even had a change to read the bill before signing it. Senator Inhofe of Oklahoma and Congressman Brad Sherman of California, among many others, told the press that the entire Congress had been threatened with martial law by the White House and the Treasury Department if they didn't pass the banker bailout bill. Moreover, the Congress and the American citizens were promised total transparency and that every dime would be accounted for, but it has not. Apparently 8.5 trillion is unaccounted for; it's not lost its stolen.

After the TARP bailout, billions were given to select banks with the intention of making money available to the public in the form of badly needed loans and investment; after selling the idea to the public and the congress, U.S. Secretary of the Treasury and former Goldman Sachs CEO Henry Paulson, changed the direction on his own to giving the money for the banks to use at their own discretion. Instead of providing credit to the public as the money was allocated for the select banks that did receive TARP money, instead, primarily used it to acquire most of the other banks and create a banking monopoly—a financial coup. Now we have the Chase Bank and Citicorp all over California.

Insurance companies also invest in large projects and investments, serving as corporate bankers with their reserves. Global insurance premiums grew by 3.4 percent in 2008 to reach $4.3 trillion. In 2008 Europe had a premium income of $1,753 billion, North America $1.346 billion and Asia $933 billion. The United States and Japan represent 7 percent of the world's population, and account for 40 percent of the world's insurance. The current merger trend in financial services has also brought more of the insurance industry under the banking cartel, as banks are now allowed to own insurance companies and other financial services that used to be forbidden by law. The courts keep overturning the laws that regulated the industry for us.

TARP

The Troubled Asset Relief Program or TARP was signed into law by president George W. Bush on October 2008; it allows the United States government to purchase assets and equity from financial institutions in order to strengthen financial institutions. Of the $245 billion invested in U.S. banks through TARP over $169 billion has been paid back, and companies like GM, AIG, and Citigroup are buying back the Treasury's stake.

TARP allows the United States Department of the Treasury to purchase or insure up to $700 billion of "troubled assets" such as collateralized debt obligations like mortgages, derivatives, and other defaulted debt. The primary recipients of TARP funds include, by largest recipient: Citigroup, Bank of America, AIG, JPMorgan Chase, Wells Fargo, GMAC Financial Services, General Motors, Goldman Sachs, Morgan Stanley, PNC Financial Group, U.S. Bancorp, Chrysler, Capital One Financial, Regions Financial Corporation, American Express, and Bank of New York Mellon Corp. The cartel paid itself, the rest were purchased cheap, and the whole Treasury was filled with Goldman Sachs executives to insure the proper allocation of funding or investment.

Much of this TARP has already been paid back, and all appear to be on schedule to pay back the funds in full. However, as of March of 2009 none of the publically traded banks had yet bought back their warrants from the Treasury. According to the terms of the agreement, the banks that received the funds can either negotiate to buy back the warrants at fair market price, or the U.S. Treasury can sell the warrants to third-party investors. Warrants are call options that would enable the holders to sell their shares on the open market. The American Bankers Association (ABA) has lobbied the Congress hard to cancel the warrants owned to the taxpayers and withhold any and all regulations or restrictions on their industry or activity. Canceling the warrants amounts to a subsidy to the banking industry and yet another case of how profits become privatized and losses become socialized; ultimately the taxpayer pays the price and the rich get richer.

The Emergency Economic Stabilization Act of 2008 was originally proposed by U.S. Treasury Secretary Henry Paulson, to bailout the U.S. financial system. Henry Paulson was CEO of Goldman Sachs, one of the leading causes of the crises through irresponsible trading as well as one of the few financial institutions that received TARP money.

Goldman Sachs was one of the leaders in reversing the "**net capital rule**" that required brokerages to hold reserve capital that limited their leveraged positions and risk exposure. In 1999 the **Gramm-Leach-Bliley Act** put the parent holding company of each of the big American brokerages beyond the American Securities and Exchange Commission oversight; now the banking industry allows "voluntary" inspections of their parent and subsidiary holding and in September 2008 the voluntary regulation was ended. We've got the leaders of those needing to be regulated becoming the heads of the regulatory agencies, and lobbyists filling key positions in cabinets that should be providing oversight for the publics interest, the American people are being very misled; it's criminal.

The Financial Crisis Inquiry Commission was created as part of the Fraud Enforcement and Recovery Act (Public Law 111-21) passed by Congress and signed by president Barak Obama in May 2009 to: "examine the causes, domestic, and global, of the current financial and economic crisis in the United States." This independent ten-member panel was composed of private citizens from the financial community, Chaired by Phil Angelides, they summarize their findings as follows:

> The Commission concluded that this crisis was avoidable - the result of human actions, inactions, and misjudgments. Warnings were ignored. The greatest tragedy

would be to accept the refrain that no one could have seen this coming and thus nothing could have been done. If we accept this notion, it will happen again.

The Financial Crisis Inquiry Commission also identified several specific areas to be addressed:

It found widespread failures in financial regulation; dramatic breakdowns in corporate governance; excessive borrowing and risk-taking by households and Wall Street; policy makers who were ill prepared for the crisis; and systemic breaches in accountability and ethics at all levels.

Detractors feel the commission oversimplified the problems and ignore the global nature of the problem but acknowledge that there was a credit bubble. The report also shows how compensation within the financial sectors has skyrocketed past other sectors in the past decade, more than doubling or twice that of other industries. The amount that Wall Street executives pay themselves has reached an all time high.

In July 21, 2010 President Barack Obama signed into law the **Dodd-Frank Wall Street Reform and Consumer Protection Act** to create sweeping reforms within government agencies and within the financial services industry. The outline of this bill includes consolidating regulatory agencies, eliminating the national thrift charter and an oversight council to evaluate systemic risk; regulation of financial markets, including increased transparency of derivatives; creating uniform standards of protection for consumers and investors; giving the Federal Reserve authorization from the Treasury for extensions of credit in "unusual or exigent circumstances"; and proposals to improve accounting and regulation of credit rating agencies. Later Paul Vocker, former Federal Reserve Board chairman and current chair of the President's Economic Recovery Advisory Board added to restrict United States banks from making certain speculative investments that are not on behalf of their customers.

All these protections and regulations are a step forward in managing our economy, but the political cycles and changing administrations tends to deregulate the industry within a few years again, and it's rarely covered well in the press. We've seen this cycle of regulation and deregulation of the financial industry, and each time we deregulate in response to lobbying pressure in Washington we end up with another economic recession. During the 1980s and 1990s we had what was called the **Savings and Loan** crisis, where over 747 savings and loan associations failed, and the U.S. taxpayer paid $124.6 billion to bail out the industry, which both times had just been deregulated.

Commercial and Investment Banking

The Banking Act of 1933 established the Federal Deposit Insurance Corporation (FDIC) and introduced banking reforms, particularly the control of speculation, and implemented the Glass-Steagall Act, which divided the roles of commercial banking and investment banking. Commercial banking, or business banking, provides checking accounts, saving accounts, money market accounts, and consumer and business credit. Investment banks speculate on investments and in capital and equity markets and assume much greater risk as a result. However, in November 1999, the **Gramm-Leach-Bliley Act** repealed these safeguards, which, again, created irresponsible lending which led to the collapse of our financial markets.

This repeal enabled lenders like Citigroup, in 1999 the largest U.S. bank by assets, to underwrite and trade instruments such as mortgage-backed securities, collateralized debt obligations, and structured investment vehicles (SIVs). After mortgage and other loans are made, they are bundled into pools of loans and sold off to institutional investors, mostly funds. The year before the repeal, the more risky subprime loans represented just 5 percent of mortgage loans, but at the peak of the credit crisis in 2008 it was approaching 30 percent. Major causes of the economic collapse include adjustable rate mortgages, mark-to-market accounting, and the Basel Accords.

After a loan is made, why should the rate go up? If the cost of money goes up, future loans would naturally also go up. However, after a loan is made why should the rate increase at the arbitrary decision of those who are profiting by you? As rates climbed during the recession, an increasing number of home owners could no longer afford to pay their mortgages and then when their inflated home values adjusted, many home owners discovered that they owed more than their homes were worth. Most mortgage lenders make their profits off the loan fees charged up front, which cover basic operational costs, but the real money is made on "the back end" when the lending institutions sell their loans in bundles of hundreds of millions.

Generally, once the loan is sold, the lender doesn't need to worry about foreclosures, so they are incentivized to make increasingly riskier loans (later buy-back agreements were developed, so banks did have to share at least part of the risk). Profits are privatized and losses are socialized. Mark-to-market or fair market accounting allowed financial institutions to make values on their balance sheet change frequently as market conditions change, as opposed to looking at book value based on the original cost/price of an asset or liability, and this has led to accounting fraud on a massive scale, Enron being one of the most visible examples.

Over-The-Counter (OTC) Derivatives

Derivatives are essentially insurance contracts—a formula-based financial contract between buyers and sellers that are not traded on exchanges and are not regulated by the government. They have proven dangerous again and again but make financial institutions lots of money, unless they fail, which they often do. The banks make profits, but when they fail the taxpayer has to pay the costs and this has bankrupted many government agencies that use them. They've been used to try to stabilize markets, or hedge against market volatility— and that is needed—but the derivative contract is a scam. If we had better regulation we would not need them. Most investors don't really even understand how they work. An **interest rate swap** is a derivative that one party exchanges a steam of interest payments for another party's stream of cash flows. Hedgers use interest rate swaps to manage their fixed or floating assets and liabilities. These instruments are also used by speculators to replicate unfunded bond exposures to profit from changes in interest rates.

Interest rate swaps were originally created to allow multinational companies to evade exchange controls, and are typically used today to hedge against or speculate on changes in interest rates. Interest rate swaps are also very popular because of the arbitrage opportunities they provide; because of the varying levels of creditworthiness between companies, there is often a positive quality spread differential that allows both parties to benefit from the interest rate swap. The unregulated derivative market has been sighted by economists as one of the major contributing causes of the great recession. The Bank for International Settlements reports that interest rate swaps are the second largest component of the global OTC derivative market; in December of 2009 the national amount outstanding in OTC interest rate swaps was $342 trillion; it's unregulated.

The Eurodollar

Eurodollars are time deposits of U.S. dollars in bank accounts held outside the laws of the United States; originally the term applied to U.S. money held in Europe, whereas now it refers to any dollars held in any country outside the United States. Eurodollar deposits are a cheaper source of funds because they were free of reserve requirements and deposit insurance assessments, and they can avoid regulation. Eurodollar futures are a way for companies and banks to lock in an interest rate today, for money it intends to borrow or lend in the future. Through the Chicago Mercantile Exchange (CME) a contract with a "face value" can be leveraged and traded with a margin based on LIBOR rates. The London Interbank Offered Rate (LIBOR) is set by the British Bankers Association.

Eurodollars are also used in "sweeps." By law banks are not allowed to pay interest on corporate checking accounts, but larger banks get around this provision by transferring funds from corporate checking accounts into overnight investment options to earn interest on those funds, typically transferring those funds to offshore branches of the bank.

Money held **offshore** in accounts that are not taxed amounted to over $11.5 trillion. Many defense contractors and oil companies working overseas create offshore companies to avoid paying United States taxes, it's also how a lot of members of Congress get paid. These shelters typically only benefit a few, the rich, and cheat the public of tax revenue for the benefit all the people—both America's revenues and those of the host country. The offshore tax haven and U.S. tax laws regarding them serve the top 1 percent and is why most of the most wealthy pay little or no taxes.

Equity Markets

Stock and other forms of equity in public corporations, as well as bonds and other securities, are traded in open markets, under competitive bidding, open disclosure and regulated market conditions.

Stock exchanges serve multiple roles in our economy, including raising capital for corporate expansion by raising capital through the selling of shares of stock; mobilizing capital for investment in industry to spur economic growth; sharing wealth with investors; corporate governance; supporting the liquidity of government bonds which, in turn, enables the creation of more credit; and serving as an overall indicator of economic well being.

From the World Federation of Exchanges, the largest Stock Exchanges as of November 2010 include:

Major Stock Exchanges

Rank	Economy	Exchange	Market Capitalization
1	United States	New York	$13041 Billion
2	United States	NASDAQ	$3649
3	Japan	Tokyo	$3542
4	UK	London	$3354
5	Hong Kong	Hong Kong	$2696
6	Europe	Euronext	$2695
7	China	Shanghai	$2681
8	Canada	Toronto	$2002
9	India	Bombay	$1540
10	India	National	$1503

The total global market capitalization, from all exchanges including the smaller ones not posted here, amount to $51751 billion.

Black and Gray Markets

In addition to the public markets for goods and services, equity and debt, the world also has a thriving black market; this includes trade in drug trafficking, arms trafficking, prostitution, and even tips. Most of these transactions are not published statistics and are unreliable. Using the Black Market Products Index at Havoscope from 2010, the Black Market is represented as follows:

Marijuana	$142 billion
Prostitution	$108 billion
Counterfeiting	$100 billion
Counterfeit Drugs	$75 billion
Prescription Drugs	$73 billion
Cocaine	$70 billion
Opium & Heroin	$65 billion
Web Video Piracy	$60 billion
Software Piracy	$53 billion
Cigarette Smuggling	$50 billion

This black market is $796 billion, not including arms sales. In developed economies like the United States, Japan, or Switzerland the shadow economies represent less than 10 percent of the GDP (using 1990s data), whereas other European countries the percentage moves into 20 percent and higher, and in developing countries the black market may represent over 50 percent of their economy.

The gray market typically refers to commodities that are traded underground, under the table or otherwise avoid paying taxes or contributing to Social Security or Medicare. This is sometimes referred to as the "hidden economy." These commodities typically include automobiles, cell phones, computer games, DVDs, pharmaceuticals, pianos, electronics, broadcasting, and intellectual property, it also includes tips and paying for labor under the table.

Food and Agriculture

The United States is a net exporter of food. The 2007 census indicated there were 2.1 million farms in the United States, covering over 922 million acres. The leading agricultural products include, by order: corn, milk, soybeans, wheat, sugar beets, potatoes, tomatoes, cattle, oranges, sorghum, and rice. Globally rice, corn, and wheat provide 60 percent of human food supply. In 2009 China was the largest agricultural producer, followed by the European Union, India, and the United States. The United States controls almost half the world grain exports, and since 1948 has increased its production through automation 2.6 times according to the IMF. According to the *CIA Factbook 2008*, 40 percent of the world's laborers are employed in agriculture, making it by far the most common occupation.

The industrial age gave birth to new methods of agriculture that have radically changed farming; innovation in agricultural machinery and farming methods, genetic technology, techniques for achieving economies of scale in production, the creation of new markets for consumption, and world trade have greatly enhanced agricultural production and profit. Twenty years ago a farmer could harvest twenty bushels of wheat per acre, and now they can produce 200 bushels an acre. The identification of nitrogen, potassium, and phosphorus (NPK) as a critical factor in growth let to the manufacturing of synthetic fertilizers; the discovery of vitamins, and their role in animal nutrition, antibiotics, and vaccines also led to increased yields, as did the role of pesticides. Now, most of our food is manufactured. However, some of these same innovations have also led to human health risks and environmental concerns that often get pushed aside because of lobbying efforts of the largest industrial corporations who's focus is on profits not human health concerns.

Moreover, most of the food people eat in Western countries is processed, high fat, high in complex carbohydrates, salt, and refined sugar, and is not healthy for human consumption over the long term. Obesity, heart disease, and diabetes have all been linked to the new foods created during the industrial revolution. Less live food, with less nutrition in the food, has given rise to the organic agriculture. Over 30 percent of the agricultural land developed in the United States is being used to grow corn; 80 to 90 percent of the products sold in supermarkets have a corn or soybean base (typically both). The high starch food is made into numerous byproducts—mostly sugars—that are in almost all processed foods, such as: high fructose corn syrups, moltodextrin, di-glycerides, xanthangum, ascorbic acid, fructose, sorbitol, calcium stearate, and saccharin. These corn sugars are loaded in processed food; it's cheap and people have adapted to wanting lots of sugar in their diet. The market for organic products has grown from nothing in 1990 to $51 billion in 2008, and now the organic farming industry is being taken over by industrial farming corporations who control the market. Having fewer small farms and bigger conglomerates is changing the face of agriculture today.

Only a handful of corporations are controlling our food system in the United States; it's another monopoly. Four beef producers—Tyson, Gargill, Swift, and National Beef—control 80 percent of the market according to the recent documentary called *Food Inc*. The same holds true for pork and other livestock or crops. Chickens are now raised and slaughtered in half the time, and are now twice as big. We can produce more and more cheaply, but we are also now under the control of another monopoly and historically this hurts society in the long run with higher prices, fewer choices, and less value; ultimately, competition is driven out, selection is diminished, and prices go up whenever you have a monopoly.

The United States government used to protect its citizens with regulations, but lobbying efforts have loosened regulations and restrictions. This corporate favoritism, including earmarks and subsidies, has driven most small farmers out of business, diminished employment, and ultimately hurt the economy. The former chief of staff at the Food and Drug Administration (FDA), had previously been the leading lobbyist for the beef industry, and another former head had been vice president of the National Food Processors Association. According to Food, Inc.: "In 1972 the FDA conducted approximately 50,000 food safety inspections. In 2006 the FDA conducted 9,164."

Obesity is literally a national epidemic, and now one in three Americans born after 2000 are expected to contract the early onset of diabetes; among minorities it's one in two. This is directly attributable to fast food, processed food, and lack of proper live foods from nature and lack of exercise.

Obesity is also linked to heart disease, cancer, osteoarthritis, and other diseases, which are all linked to the new American industrial diet. Processed foods are added value because they tend to make more money than just selling commodities like fruits and vegetables; there are higher margins and profits to be made. We eat what we are sold depending on what makes the most profit. The food that we eat is creating a national health crisis. According to Dr. Jason A. Deitch and Dr. Bob Hoffman, authors of the best-selling book *Discover Wellness*:

> With over 50 percent of personal bankruptcies related to medical debt and companies such as Starbucks spending more money on health care than coffee, America's present health care crisis is making America sick.

The seed monopoly. If you control the seed you control agriculture, and over the span of two decades Monsanto Corporation has accumulated around 650 key plant-related biotech patents. By 2004 Monsanto had a 29 percent share of all research and development in the biotech industry. These new genetically altered and patented seeds do not reproduce, so, whereas a farmer would normally recover seeds from one harvest for the next season's crops, now a farmer must go back and buy more seeds making them dependent on Monsanto. Moreover, these genetically altered seeds produce pollen, which is introduced to crops not grown with Monsanto's seeds and they pick up the genetic imprints of the new seed strains in a process called cross-pollination.

Thus, all our food is beginning to be produced from seed strains coming from Monsanto, so they are literally trying to control the world's food resources and claim these slightly altered foods as their own. In 2008 Monsanto's revenues were $11.365 billion, they dominate the seed industry, as well as the herbicides and pesticides industries and are creating the largest agricultural monopoly in the world.

Today, the most powerful and important industries—banking, energy, and agriculture—are all dominated by monopolies, each of which share common financial interests. Never before has so much power been in the hands of so few people. In the words of Henry Kissinger:

Who controls the food supply controls the people; Who controls energy can control whole continents; Who controls money controls the world.

The Dutch East India Company and Multinational Corporations

The Dutch East India Company or United East Indian Company (VOC in Dutch) was the world's first multinational corporation and the first to issue stock; it also had a quasi-governmental powers such as the ability to wage war, imprison and execute convicts, negotiate treaties, coin money, and establish colonies. Between 1602 and 1796 the company sent almost a million Europeans to work in trade with Asia and over 2.5 million tons were traded on over 4,785 ships. The competing British East India Company carried about one-fifth the cargo on 2,690 ships. In the beginning profits averaged 18 percent of total revenues, and later dropped to 10 percent with the competition of other European traders. One of the main imports from Asia in the beginning was pepper.

The Portuguese had captured much of the spice trade and the Dutch began trading spices to meet Europe's increasing demand. **The British East India Company** made a lucrative business of going to Africa to purchase slaves that they sold to the United States to work the cotton fields. The cotton was then exported to Great Britain to manufacture into cloth, which was then sold to India (which was prohibited from manufacturing cloth).India paid for the cloth and other Western goods with the opium they were growing for the British traders, and that opium was traded by the British monopoly to the Chinese, who they intentionally got hooked on the opium. This led to the Opium Wars between the British and the Chinese, 1839-1860, which created distrust between the East and the West that continues today.

America loves substances, it began its industry growing and selling tobacco, we are a major producer of the world's alcohol which is one of the most common substances sold in the world, and the pharmaceutical industry is one of the largest and most powerful industries in the world. In 2006 global spending on prescription drugs topped $643 billion, and the United States accounts for almost half the global pharmaceutical industry. Drugs are still one of the most profitable industries in the world, legal, or otherwise, and America is by far the largest consumer of these mind altering substances.

One of the biggest multinational, multi-industry, trading economies today involves the trade of arms for oil in the Middle East, and its financing and aid. The United States subsidizes the arms industry by tying military contracts to financial aid or contracting with American companies. All oil-producing nations need bigger militaries to protect their nations assets and this, in turn, helps support the United States **defense** industry.

It is estimated that over $1.5 trillion dollars a year is spent on the procurement of arms internationally; that's 2.7 percent of the world GDP. As of 2008 the United States represents 41.5 percent of the world's spending, followed by China 5.8 percent, France 4.5 percent, United Kingdom 4.5 percent and Russia at 4.0 percent; the largest exporters are the United States, Russia, Germany, France, and United Kingdom; the largest importers are India, Singapore, Malaysia, Greece, South Korea, Pakistan, Algeria, United States, Australia, Turkey, Saudi Arabia, and the United Arab Emirates.

In addition to governmental military expenditures, more states, corporations, and NGOs are using **Private Military Companies** (PMCs) to replace or support military operations, including security, escorts, risk assessments or threat analysis, information services, espionage, and security training. The Center for Public Integrity reported that since 1994, the U.S. Defense Department entered into 3,601 contracts worth over $300 billion. During the 1991 Gulf War the ratio of military personnel to contractors was fifty to one, but during the Iraq War the U.S. hired over 190,000 contractors—more than the total American military presence during the Iraq surge in 2007.

In Afghanistan, the ratio of military personnel to PMCs is almost one to one; there are around 100,000 civilian contractors, and almost as many uniformed soldiers working in Afghanistan and the United States is paying for it all, and a lot of ex-government officials, lobbyists, and investors are getting rich.

The Largest Corporations

As corporations continue to consolidate, rolling up into increasingly larger conglomerates and crossing national boundaries, their economic strength begins to dominate the industries and markets they serve until they are bigger and stronger than most countries. With that strength they dominate other countries and their economies and politics.

Fortune magazine compiles data on corporate performance, and an overview of these multinationals serves as a snapshot of the world economy and who runs it. Of the top 1,000 industrial corporations of the world over 450 were located in Europe, 195 were in the United States and 80 were in Japan.

Fortune Global 500 - Top 10 List 2010 (By Sales)

Rank	Company	Country	Industry
1	Wall-Mart	United States	Retail
2	Shell Oil	Netherlands/UK	Oil
3	Exxon Mobil	United States	Oil
4	BP	United Kingdom	Oil
5	Toyota	Japan	Automobile
6	Japan Post	Japan	Holding Co.
7	Sinopec	China	Oil
8	State Grid	China	Power
9	AXA	France	Insurance
10	China Petro	China	Oil

Another valuable indicator of industrial strength within an economy is to look at the capacity to produce and the infrastructure within the economy. *Fortune* also breaks down the Global 500 largest companies by the number of them within a country. In 2010:

Number of Global 500 by Country

Rank	Nation	#Companies
1	United States	139
2	Japan	71
3	China	46
4	France	39

5	Germany	37
6	United Kingdom	29
7	Switzerland	15
8	Netherlands	13
9	Canada	11
10	Italy	11

Top United States Corporations

The *Fortune* 500 top industrial corporations in the United States for 2010 are:

1	Wal-Mart Stores	Retail
2	Exxon Mobil	Oil
3	Chevron	Oil
4	General Electric	Manufacturing
5	Bank of America	Banking
6	Conoco-Philips	Oil
7	AT&T	Communications
8	Ford Motor	Automotive
9	J.P. Morgan Chase	Banking
10	Hewlett-Packard	Manufacturing

However, all these industries depend on money; money is what drives industry and commerce. Within a generation or two all the largest conglomerates will share interests and financing, the world is becoming one global corporation run by money and the people who control the money—the 1 percent.

One percent Verses the World

One percent of the people in this world control the entire world, and all the rest need to understand this. The greatest power for change in the world are people with a vision. When people gather together under a righteous cause like liberty, justice, or freedom, they accomplish extraordinary things. All the wars, killing, and conquest throughout world history were due to the 1 percent of the richest people in the world seeking more wealth and power. However, the greatest achievements in civilization were not achieved by the rich, but by the people themselves rising up to demand change. Christianity has its foundation in such a movement; as did the Magna Carta, the development of representative government, democracy, free markets, and free enterprise, workers rights, and civil rights; these are the result of the common man rising up seeking justice and peace.

The founding fathers and first Americans fought for the rights of every man, and it's clearly laid out in the American Bill of Rights and the Constitution. American's were not given liberty or freedom; they demanded it and were willing to die for it. Women were not given the right to vote, but they demanded it. When the women of the suffrage movement protested and marched on Washington, they were beaten, harassed, discredited in the press, and looked down on by much of the establishment. They persevered and won. Black people were not just handed their rights; they fought for them, but they shouldn't have had to. The Vietnam War dragged on for years, until the antiwar protesters got to president Nixon. Yet, the CIA and some agents of government saw these very people as enemies of the state; people who spoke up got shot, but the war ended...as it should have. The right to protest, to march, and to express grievances are not only a right of each citizen, but a duty according to our own founding fathers. This has served to spawn the world's democracies and all the progressive changes that have served mankind.

During the last fifty years, the quality of life for most people has been diminishing. The rich are getting richer and more powerful than ever, while more and more people are going deeper into debt, and aren't able to accumulate wealth, or enjoy true freedom. The middle class is being squeezed into servitude through debt, and economic policies that don't serve them. The primary reason for this injustice is because the average person is uninformed and unaware of how their lives are affected by these economic forces and the people who are invisible to most of us.

In an review essay by Robert C. Lieberman in the January/ February 2011 issue of *Foreign Affairs* called "Why the Rich Are Getting Richer," where he reviews the book *Winner-Take-All Politics: How Washington Made the Rich Richer* by Jacob S. Hacker and Paul Pierson, he explains:

> Since the late 1970s, a number of important policy changes have tilted the economic playing field towards the rich. Congress has cut tax rates on high incomes repeatedly and has relaxed the tax treatment of capital gains and other investment income, resulting in windfall profits for the wealthiest Americans.

And:

> [C]orporate governance policies have enabled corporations to lavish extravagant pay on their top executives regardless of their companies' performance; and the deregulation of financial markets has allowed banks and other financial institutions to create even more Byzantine financial instruments that further enrich wealthy managers and investors while exposing homeowners and pensioners to ruinous risks.

All we have to do is look at the facts: unemployment is approaching 10 percent in the United States, the highest level in over thirty years; foreclosures have forces millions of Americans out of their homes and offices; and real income has fallen faster and further than at any time since the Great Depression. Yet, the wealthiest Americans, among them the very people who led the speculative practices that brought about the financial meltdown and those who were supposed to protect us, got richer. According to Jacob Hacker and Paul Pierson in *Winner-Take-All Politics: How Washington Made the Rich Richer*, in 2009, the average income of the top five percent of earners went up, while on average everyone else's income went down.

In Congressman Ron Paul's book *End the Fed*, he lucidly explains how the average person is losing through the current economic policies of the Federal Reserve:

> One only needs to reflect on the dramatic decline in the value of the dollar that has taken place since the Fed was established in 1913. The goods and services you could buy for $1.00 in 1913 now cost nearly $20.00. Another way to look at this is from the perspective of the purchasing power of the dollar itself. It has fallen to less than $0.05 of its 1913 value. We might say that the government and its banking cartel have together stolen

$0.95 of every dollar as they have pursued a relentlessly inflationary policy.

The more complacent and inactive our society becomes, the more we are taken advantage of: the more freedoms we lose, the fewer jobs we have, the more debt we are burdened with, the higher taxes we pay, the more wars are fought, and more people die. Life gets worse for all but a privileged few. Only when people realize that they have been asleep, will they truly awaken. As we collectively awaken, we can create the world as we would have it—one we each can find prosperity, happiness, and peace. The world has the resources for it, and we only need the vision to create it.

The people in control don't want to lose control, so a vigilant watch is kept to ensure our complicity. In 1949 the dystopian novelist George Orwell wrote a famous book called *1984* about an oligarchic corporate government in perpetual war ruled by a single interest—Big Brother that is constantly watching and controlling every human thought and action. In this fictional world, pervasive government surveillance and incessant public mind control and propaganda enables the state to control the masses; it's spookily similar to what's happening now.

Homeland Security and The Patriot Act

As noted earlier, every e-mail and action on the Internet, every call made, every communication through electronic medium is being tracked by the United States government. All the money coming into or out of accounts is tracked by the government, all your purchases, what you like, and where you go all on record electronically. Your health, habits, relationships, wealth, work, entertainment, friends, and resources are all at the fingertips of a select few. Face recognition software is being used in video cameras in transportation hubs, public and private structures, and from the sky with satellites, and it can now recognize a human face on the ground from space. Global positioning satellites not only help guide you to places you might want to go, they also keep track of where you are going, or have been. With massive supercomputers all this information interacts to create composites of everyone, digitally. More than ever in the history of the world, we are being watched and studied; our thoughts are molded and most of our choices programmed through engineered consent, and we don't even realize it.

The USA PATRIOT Act was signed into law in October 2001 by president George W. Bush to dramatically reduce restrictions on law enforcement agencies' ability to search telephone, e-mail, medical, financial, and other records; ease restrictions on foreign intelligence gathering within the United States; expand the Treasury's authority to regulate financial transactions, particularly those involving foreign individuals and entities; and broadened the discretion of law enforcement and immigration authorities in detaining and monitoring immigrants suspected of terrorism-related acts.

ADVISE - Analysis, Dissemination, Visualization, Insight, and Semantic Enhancement - is a program used within the U.S. Department of Homeland Security to data mine massive amounts of digital data to assess threats. The data can be from financial records, phone calls, e-mails, blog entries, Web site searches, and other forms of electronic transmission and storage. Officially, the program was scraped once it came to light in the press. The U.S. government, through DARPA, has also created the **Information Awareness Office** (IAO) to develop surveillance technology to track terrorists, including Human Identification at a Distance (HumanID), cameras that can identify you and track you; Evidence Extraction and Link Discovery (EELD), which can search and identify Internet traffic patterns and know who's talking to who; Genisys, which enables the analysis of "ultra-large, all-source information repositories," (it basically cross checks information across multiple data sources); Scalable Social Network Analysis (SSNA), which tracks social networking; Futures Markets Applied to Prediction (FutureMAP) is used to predict human behavior in possible future events, and many others. The ECHELON program intercepts radio, satellite, microwave, cellular, and fiber-optic signals to collect and analyze private information passing through these public mediums.

As a part of building the Department of Homeland Security, a whole new set of sweeping changes have been made to how intelligence is gathered, and how investigations, arrests, detentions, and prosecutions are made. For instance, the **Bank Secrecy Act** (BSA) through subtitle B, includes granting the Board of Governors of the Federal Reserve System power to authorize personnel to act as law enforcement officers to protect the premises, grounds, property, and personnel of any U.S. Federal Reserve Bank and allowing the board to delegate this authority to U.S. Federal Reserve Bank. The Fed can now command its own private army.

Under the Bush administration the **Military Commissions Act of 2006** allows the president to suspend the writs of *habeas corpus*, which is the right to be brought to court to determine whether the prisoner had been lawfully imprisoned or should be released from custody, and it is granted to the American people in Article I, Section 9, clause 2 of the United States constitution, which states:

> The Privilege of the Writ of Habeas Corpus shall not be suspended, unless when in the Cases of Rebellion or Invasion the public Safety may require it.

The Military Commissions Act grants the president of the United States almost unlimited authority in establishing and conducting military commissions to try persons held by the United States and considered to be "unlawful enemy combatants" in the global war on terrorism. However, this new term "enemy combatant" that didn't exist before, appears to include any U.S. citizen deemed to be a combatant by the president and this could include those protesting wars or other government policies.

The Supreme Court summarized the concern of Americans by posing the question in its deliberations:

> Does the Constitution permit Executive officials to detain an American citizen indefinitely in military custody in the United States, hold him essentially incommunicado and deny him access to council, with no opportunity to question the factual basis for his detention before any impartial tribunal...

In *Hamdi* v. *Rumsfeld* the verdict was mixed but the Supreme Court ruled that the U.S. government has the power to hold American citizens and foreign nationals without charges or trial, but that detainees can challenge their treatment in U.S. courts. The Supreme Court has also recently removed the restrictions on the campaign contributions corporations can make to political candidates or parties, so now any conglomerate can buy as many votes as they need, purchase as much air time on television as they need, or lobby without restraint; this is how the wealthiest 1 percent of the world's population control the world. Those who control the money rule the government, not the voters.

Representation

The United States is still one of the only industrialized nations left using the "electoral college" voting system; the electoral college was necessary during a time when going throughout the colonies on horse to collect all the votes would be impractical, now every citizens vote can be counted in minutes. What most Americans don't realize is their vote does not elect a president; someone within the two controlling parties is elected to vote on your behalf, but these electors are political positions, and electors frequently vote different than the constituents that they are supposed to represent. Candidates for elector are nominated by their state political parties in the months before Election Day. Most citizens don't even know who is chosen to cast the vote on their behalf, or even know if their elector did vote on their behalf. What you punched in your ballot is not what determines who is president or vice president; the electors' vote is what counts.

The elections of 1876, 1888, and 2000 produced an Electoral College winner who did not receive the plurality of the nationwide popular vote; in other words, who most Americans voted for did not become president, but, rather, whoever receives the most Electoral College votes wins. Thus, Americans are disenfranchised from the electoral process.

During the 2000 presidential election between Vice President Al Gore and George W. Bush, it was determined that Al Gore actually received the most popular votes, but George Bush received the most electoral college votes. Bush won the election (notwithstanding the voter fraud and miscount issues that were never fully resolved).

Continuity of Government

Continuity of government (COG) or continuity of operations is the principal of establishing procedures that allow a government to continue its essential operations in case of a nuclear war or other catastrophic event. Most industrialized nations have some form of continuity of government program. The United States has bunkers located at strategic locations for key government and executive personnel; the publicized ones include Raven Rock Mountain, Mount Weather, Camp David, the Greenbrier, Cheyenne Mountain, Strategic Command, as well as airborne command centers. The National Security and Homeland Security Presidential Directive 51 gives power to the president to execute procedures for continuity of government in the event of a "catastrophic emergency" as determined by the president. The new plan also empowers the president to issue marshal law (military force) against citizens of the United States when deemed necessary, including preventing or stopping public peaceful demonstrations.

In July 2007 U.S. Representative and Homeland Security Committee member Peter DeFazio made a request to examine the classified Continuity Annexes, which describe the details of the plan, and he was denied access to the document by the White House on the basis of national security, even though he obviously has a security clearance as the representative for Homeland Security. Later both Bernie Thompson who was chairman of the Homeland Security Committee and Chris Carney who is chairman of the Homeland Security oversight subcommittee were both also denied access after a formal written request. They simply refused the Congress, as the CIA periodically does; there's another level of government within our government.

Readiness Exercise 1984 (Rex 84) is a contingency plan written by Lieutenant Colonel Oliver North of the National Security Council and White House Aide under president Ronald Reagan, to suspend the United States Constitution, declare martial law, place military commanders in charge of state and local government, and detain large numbers of American citizens who were deemed to be "national security threats" in the event that the president declared a national emergency. During the Iran-Contra Hearings in 1987 Congressman Jack Brooks asked Colonel North about his continuity of government plan, but was told by committee chairman Senator Daniel Inouye that it could not be discussed in open session and suggested that answers to that question be discussed in executive sessions that the public would not be privy to.

Operation Garden Plot is a U.S. Army plan to respond to domestic civil disturbances within the United States, where the military would be used to suppress or eliminate protests, marches or any civil disobedience. In testimony given by Major General Richard C. Alexander, executive director of the National Guard Association of the United States, during a Senate Appropriations Committee Hearing on Homeland Defense in April 11, 2002, he stated:

> Oversight of these homeland security missions should be provided by the National Guard Bureau based on the long-standing Garden Plot model in which National Guard units are trained and equipped to support civil authorities in crowd control and civil disturbance missions.

The Federal Bureau of Investigation (FBI) also has a number of programs designed to control the U.S. public, the best known is **COINTELPRO** (Counterintelligence Program) whose aim is surveillance, infiltrating, discrediting, and disrupting domestic political organizations. COINTELPRO tactics include: discrediting targets through psychological warfare, planting false reports in the media, smearing through forged letters, harassment, wrongful imprisonment, extralegal violence, and assassination under the auspices of "national security." According to FBI records, 85 percent of COINTELPRO resources targeted what they considered "subversive" groups, including groups labeled communist or socialist, as well as civil rights movements, Dr. Martin Luther King, Jr., Southern Christian Leadership Conference, NAACP, Students for Democracy, the National Lawyers Guild (who questioned the legality of their program), antiwar advocates or demonstrators, and women's rights leaders.

In 1975 the United States Senate Select Committee to Study Governmental Operations with Respect to Intelligence Activities, chaired by Senator Frank Church held a series of hearings to determine the extent of U.S. government involvement is assassinations and covert operations against citizens of the United States. In the final report of the Select Committee, much of which has still not been released, it determined:

> Many of the techniques used would be intolerable in a democratic society even if all of the targets had been involved in violent activity, but COINTELPRO went far beyond that...the Bureau conducted a sophisticated vigilante operation aimed squarely at preventing the exercise of First Amendment rights of speech and association, on the theory that preventing the growth of dangerous groups and the propagation of dangerous ideas would protect the national security and deter violence.

A Government within the Government

The Federal Reserve lies at the heart of the global economy, and with the support of the United States military they dominate the world politics and global economic conditions, yet they work in secret for the world's 1 percent most wealthy. They essentially work as a government within the government; and act outside the laws and will of the American people. According to congressman Ron Paul who has worked on the House Banking Committee:

> There is essentially no oversight, no audit, and no control. And the Fed is protected by the Federal Reserve Act. That's why the Federal Reserve chairman has no obligation to answer questions that relate to Federal Open Market Committee meetings and actions taken in collusion with other central banks. Trillions of dollars

can be created and injected into the economy with no obligation by the Fed to reveal who benefits. Lawsuits and freedom of information demands will not shake this information loose.

The concern for all citizens is that a small elite of banking and business leaders dominates world governance. In a speech made by president John F. Kennedy just before his assassination, he spoke to American people warning of a conspiracy within the government and how they were using the excuse of national security to censor and conceal, stating:

> And there is a very grave danger, that announced need for increased security will be seized upon by those anxious to expand its means to the very limits of official censorship and concealment that I intend not to permit to the extent it is within my control.

Enlightened Capitalism

The founding fathers of the United States saw themselves living in the Age of Enlightenment, and their ideas were enlightened. There vision is still attainable and the opportunity has arisen. This economy can turn around very easily; the world has the resources, technology, and skill within the labor market, it's all a matter of who controls the money. Money is the instrument of power. It can and is used for greater good, but it can also be, and is, manipulated for selfish gain and profit. We need to be wiser, and we need to make some changes. I have some suggestions.

You will need to use lateral thinking to move away from how you've been conditioned to think it has to be, to looking at other possibilities even if they seem impractical at first.

Talking Points and Action Steps

1

Realization. We need to realize that we have been asleep and that we need to awaken. Each citizen needs to take some responsibility for the financial situation we are in and improve the situation by learning more about how the world really works. This goes for the people of every nation, but Americans share an additional responsibility as the remaining superpower of the world to lead the world economy. We can create a world that shares resources and lives in peace, or continue to allow the privileged few to rule the world out of power and greed and keep citizens enslaved through ignorance and debt. Moreover, the founding fathers of the United States warned us of this very situation we are in now, and gave us a solution: we have to question, reason, and rebel. We need to wake up and realize we've been asleep; we need to enlighten.

2

Questioning. We need to question more. If history has taught us one thing, it's that businessmen and politicians lie; we can't believe everything they tell us, and we need to ask more questions and go to direct data sources to get answers. We need to demand straight answers from business and government alike, and consider other perspectives in order to gain greater perspective. Choosing sides isn't an answer.

We can't rely on the media either; we must recognize the role the media plays in propaganda, left or right, especially approaching the prospect of war. Our regulators are not doing their job, we have lobbyists running our government, a consciousness of corruption is the norm at the highest levels of government and business but only because we allow it. Each citizen must develop his or her ability to think independently, to question what he or she hears, and to not be too quick to form an opinion or take a side without some independent research and reflection. It takes more effort to question, but this is exactly what is needed.

3

End Lobbying. Lobbying is bribery. Whenever you give money to someone he or she is beholding to you; almost all our representatives receive millions from corporations and lobbyists in one form or another, and turn around and earmark millions to those same corporations and special interests that support them. This is just wrong. Representatives of the people should not be taking money from corporations or special interests. Politicians need money for media primarily. The airwaves belong to the people and qualified candidates should receive free airtime. Campaigns should not be bought, we'd have better leaders if they were not beholding to their financial backers and sponsors. Right now the royalty rule through the money they bribe representatives with.

Corporate interests certainly need to be heard, too, and public forums for just that purpose should be created. We want business to succeed; let's do all we can to support a powerful economy. Let's talk about what we want to create as a society together. Industrial roundtables between industrial leaders and congress could spur great ideas for cooperative development, rather than behind closed-door meetings where money is exchanged under the table or when offshore accounts are created to bribe government officials.

Let's pay our representatives well, judge them by their works, and have full financial disclosure and transparency. The public media is owned by some of the most powerful corporate interests; it's the mouthpiece of business. Whoever spends the most tends to win, and that's not the best way to get good representation. At a minimum we need to remove/prevent former lobbyists from serving in the federal government or members of government from lobbying, and/or serving in positions with potential conflicts of interests, including the revolving doors in all levels of government. It breeds corruption and puts special interests ahead of the best interests of the people.

4

The Common Good. In all our decision making in business, politics, and banking, we need to ask ourselves one ethical question to distinguish right from wrong: Does it serve a common good or just benefit a few? Who truly benefits and who bears the cost? A lack of ethics in business lies at the heart of the problem. We need better role models in business and government, and stronger policing of our leadership, and greater reporting of what's really going on. Everyone needs to ask him/herself who's interest are they serving, what good are they doing, and what trust are they breaking, if any. The cases and principals in this book should be taught as ethics in every school of business and government.

5

End the Federal Reserve. Debt-based currency is inflationary, and giving control of the nation's currency to a banking Cartel has proven to benefit the few who control the system and hurt the public taxpayers and the economy in general. Money is power, and putting the power of the country and the world in the hands of a few who make decisions and take actions in secret, and don't disclose accounts or consult with those whose lives are affected is foolish. The actions of the Federal Reserve affect the lives of every person more than most actions of the president or congress, and history has clearly shown how the Fed does not work for the public good.

Causing debt to create currency is foolish, and the ultimate cause of continued economic duress. All financial transactions need to be open to the public and subject to public scrutiny.

We need a group of financial leaders that are neither politically or financially motivated to manage the currency, so it benefits the whole of the economy not just a select few, and a clear set of guidelines and action steps laid out in advance to know ahead of time if the economy moves off course what to do. We need to break the banking monopoly, and the influence it has over our government and economy. First we need to audit the Fed, so we can learn more about the cause-effect relationships from its policies, and then phase it out giving the power of the currency to the U.S. Treasury, with a independent board and complete transparency for the public in all transactions. Secrecy is at the heart of the problem, and transparency and accountability is the solution.

6

An Honest Buck. The United States Treasury should issue its own currency again based on the *assets* of the nation rather than its *liabilities*. By creating our own currency we do not need to incur debt, as no bonds or bills need to be created, thus no interest needs to be paid on debt. Therefore, the taxpayer does not bear a giant tax burden to pay off the government debt, and our currency will inflate less if we don't have to pay interest on it. This will further lower our taxes. The caveat is to circulate the proper amounts of currency, so we don't inflate it as we have in the past.

Simply replacing a debt-based currency with an asset-based currency (based on the assets of the nation including gold, silver, oil, and other natural resources) will lower our national debt, which will in turn strengthen our currency and our economy. That will in turn strengthen the world economy. Our nation has done this before with great success, but what is needed is an impartial means to regulate the money supply. Those in control of the money supply cannot be motivated by wealth, power, or politics because that has hurt us in the past. We should start gradually replacing the old debt-based money already in circulation with the new *honest bucks*, so we don't create too much money at one time and inflate the currency even more. We need to manage the growth of our currency and economy by controlling the money supply, eliminating the debt, and adding enough new money for business to grow without inflating it. We need steady consistent paced growth.

7

Managed Growth- The 5 percent Rule. Every household, business, and institution should have a plan to manage their finances and plan their future, and our nation should do the same. For a nation 2 percent annual growth is low, and 10 percent is high; a nominal 5 percent annual growth rate could serve as a baseline for growth and a goal to transit out of our depression and back into prosperity again. If our nation is growing at a 5 percent annually, that's a sign of a strong economy.

Those areas not growing need stimulation, and those experiencing a pace of growth exceeding double digits tend to get inflated. If lenders watched land values, home prices, stock and commodity prices, and other indications of value, and managed the money in circulation so cheap money no longer inflated values, we would not experience the radical boom and bust years that have repeatedly hurt the standard of living of the average citizen. Begin with the 5 percent rule of thumb. More speculative investments are still available for those with surplus capital who can afford the loss, not for citizens, or consumers, or the economy.

8

Asset-Based Lending. The United States Treasury makes capital available through the existing banking system using U.S. bucks without interest. The banks still make a fee for their services, enough for them to profit, but the loans are of principal only. As principal is paid back to the banks, that money can be lent out again when needed, keeping a more consistent supply and flow of the currency, rather than using fractional reserve banking, which inflates currency. In the case of a mortgage, the down payment still serves as the earnest money that pays the closing costs, including bank fees, and the amount borrowed is paid back in equal installments over the course of the loan. But now, instead of all the interest that is typically paid up front for the first ten years of the loan, the borrower is growing equity with each payment; he or she is creating real value, for real labor. It's real money with real value.

Moreover, since there is no interest on the loan, the monthly payments are much lower, which makes owning property more affordable. More affordable property and available credit for loans will spur home buying and building again. Lenders would need to adhere to the 5 percent growth rule so home prices do not become inflated again. We eliminate fractional reserve lending, we simply only invest where it makes good economic sense, and when creating it does not inflate the currency. As there is no debt created in an asset-based currency, the inflation is much lower. The capital created by the Treasury, in circulation in the economy, becomes an asset to the national balance sheet. It's creating real value in the economy, and to the people, not just making profit for the few. How much money is created and where it goes, needs to be guided by those not influenced by political or financial ends, and every move would have to be transparent and tested.

9

Education Investment. I agree with president Barak Obama's suggestion in his 2011 State of the Union Address to invest in the education of the nation; our competitive edge in the world economy is our education and skilled labor market. I suggest we should incentivize our best students with a free higher education, say to the top 10 percent, and offer all high school graduates that can get into college loans with no inter-est—*honest bucks*. This money being created becomes both an investment in our future, and would create a true asset to the nation. Economically we can't compete with cheap labor in world markets; we need people who can create new ideas, new products and services, new industries, and add value to the economy through their learned skills.

Innovation and an entrepreneurial spirit are our nation's greatest strengths; we have the best universities in the world; we have capital markets and a financial infrastructure to take good ideas and products to market fast and efficiently; we just need the ethical leadership to take us there and for that we must invest in our youth. History has taught us that education benefits everyone. As money borrowed for student loans is paid off on principal only loans made with *honest bucks*, that money becomes available for new loans, replenishing the money supply rather than just creating more money.

10

America, Inc. Let's make the best products in the world...in Detroit. We have up and coming industries in wind turbine and solar energy, new building materials, electric cars, batteries, etc. What could our industries use to become world leaders again? Nothing is more critical to the health of our economy than employment, so we should invest, as a country, in developing those industries where we can employ laborers at fair wages and make products competitively that can compete in world markets.

Now, many corporations will be able to find cheaper labor overseas, and so it is more profitable to manufacture abroad, but if we offered a tax incentive to industry to hire American labor we would invigorate our economy by employing more people, who would, in turn, increase our tax base. So this investment in America would ultimately increase both our GDP and tax revenues. Example: Incentivize the ailing auto industry to build all electric cars in Detroit, and in other slumped industrial cities, and hire the local labor force and those corporate profits will not be taxed for ten years. Simply put, it makes better sense to employ people to work rather than to pay out unemployment benefits.

11

Protection Under the Law. Corporations are getting so large they often have staffs of hundreds of attorneys, plus outside council, and can attack a weaker competitor, customer or client with brute force; most people or small businesses cannot bear the cost of major lawsuits. Whoever has the most money to buy lawyers typically wins. A corporation can ruin a man through lawsuits alone. Political leaders have repeatedly used the IRS to attack opponents. Moreover, presidents simply dismiss pending cases with the Department of Justice or commute a sentence at will. Our courts have recently overturned the Glass-Steagall Act, the Clayton Act, and the Sherman Antitrust Act, and now we're ruled by a cadre of monopolies that have Washington by the balls; even the limitations on contributions corporations can make has been lifted. The courts are losing the public trust.

Corporations are taking over control of government and the courts, and the citizens of our nation need to ask our Congress, president and executive branch, and our judiciary - particularly the Supreme Court, to protect us from: 1) The supreme wealth and power of the Federal Reserve and other monopolies. We are bullied by corporate interests, and we need protection so this doesn't happen ever again; 2) We ask protection that we get accurate and balanced information through the broadcasting networks with whom we've given licenses, and *transparency* in our financial transactions with the Treasury and the Federal Reserve. The people have a right to know how our nation is being governed financially and have a say in it; 3) Guarantee us our right to peacefully demonstrate, openly criticize government policies, and petition for grievances even in times of war and rebellion; 4) That the rite of *habeas corpus* not be revoked and no rights to a fair representation and public trial be revoked; 5) That all levels of government, including the CIA, FBI, Homeland Security, National Security Council, and any other body deemed necessary by the Congress testify

and comply with Congressional hearings and oversight, providing requested information in a timely manner or face jail
time like anyone else; 6) That lying by presidents, cabinets
members, or the Congress is punishable, and people caught
lying should not hold public office; and 7) The people want to
be ruled by the Constitution and the principals put forth in the
Bill of Rights, and no higher power except God himself. We
certainly do not want, or accept, an elite ruling class ruling
over the government, or us, in secret.

12

Paying Off the Debt. The key to paying off our debt is not
to create more debt to pay off the debt. We simply begin issuing *honest bucks* to replace notes and bonds that have interest; this will gradually pay down our debt and strengthen the
value of our currency. Currency inflates (is worth less) if too
much is floating through the economy, so we should stabilize
our growth at 5 percent and provide just enough money to
move the economy forward at a healthy and steady pace. As
most of the national debt is in short-term bills and bonds, the
national debt could be paid off in short order, this would bring
confidence and strength back to the currency and make the
United States more competitive in world markets. The government has to take the power of money back and regulate the
currency to benefit the whole economy.

13

Long Term Capital Gains. Short-term speculation has led
to instability in the market, and investments for short-term
gain rarely contribute to the overall growth of a company,
industry, or economy. Making a quick buck in the stock market or any market does not serve the best interests of the
nation. Conversely, long-term investments in corporations and
development can enable corporations to invest, employ, and
grow stronger and more profitable. Therefore, I suggest (1)

placing a 5 percent tax on all short-term investments, under one year; this windfall will go direct to Social Security, and (2) eliminate the long-term gains tax on all investments in the United States for individuals and companies for a period of ten years, but only for investments in the United States and in U.S. companies.

The removal of the long-term capital gains tax will primarily benefit the wealthy, but to an end that will encourage investments that would create more jobs and develop more industry and trade. While the long-term gains on investment would not be taxed, the increased income of corporations and individuals would be. Furthermore, those corporations that hire and gainfully employ new workers could be given a reprieve from corporate tax for this same ten-year period. The benefits include people working and producing, more consumer spending and taxable income, and corporations would make more profit by making long-term investments that are not taxed and would Get cheaper labor. All those new jobs bring cash flow into businesses in the communities, and to the nation at large—the whole society benefits.

14

Fair Markets. Today markets are manipulated: stock markets, bond markets, currency markets, derivative markets all have dominant participants who control movements in the market by trading equity in large volumes, often with insider knowledge. Often these pools of ownership are held in funds offshore by anonymous investors, who place bets with brokerage houses that a particular company stock or commodity price will drop at a particular point in time, then they sell off large amounts of their equity to drive the price down. In other words, they sell short.

First, these investors make money by winning their bet that the equity devalues from their actions, precipitating an equity death spiral where other investors jump on board the selling spree, and then they can buy back that same equity for a fraction of the market price. This scam recurs repeatedly. George Soros is notorious for manipulating markets for personal gain. This is one of the primary causes of our current economic collapse—our markets are manipulated and not really free. Moreover, it was this market instability that led to the derivative market, which has only created more instability.

These, and other "pump and dump" schemes need to be regulated, and not by people who come from and go back to work for the same industries they are supposed to be regulating. Investment bankers have no business working in the U.S. Treasury. This is a clear conflict of interest, and the people's interests are not being served, but rather the interests of the cartel are. All markets need to be better regulated, particularly the derivative market, with consequences that will truly deter crime.

15

Usury. The adjustable interest rate has been a devise used in banking that more than any other banking scheme has hurt the strength of our economy. One of the largest margins of profit for a bank is on those borrowers who maximize their credit—borrowing—and then make just the minimum payment possible. Most debtors never get out of this hole, they typically obtain more credit and max it out, and then if they have any equity in their home they tap into that equity like an ATM machine and lose their equity. Then, once they got you beholding to them the banks arbitrarily raise the interest rate, and you have no choice but to make those higher payments. Thus, almost every American is deeply in debt and will never get out. Almost all citizens, companies, and governments are now beholding to banks through debt. It's indentured slavery.

Moreover, after qualifying for a loan at a particular rate—credit cards, mortgages, and lines of credit—banks often raise the rate of interest, and once you've agreed to this loan you are beholding to pay that higher rate. Adjustable rates on existing loans are a primary cause of our real estate market collapse, as rates went higher the higher payments were more than many borrowers could make. Once a loan is made, why should a rate go up? New loans may need to be made at higher or lower rates as the market dictates, but with existing loans where the money is already lent and the investors are already receiving their agreed upon rate of return, there is no reason for those rates to go up. Rates only go up when banking committees such as the Federal Reserve eleventh district or the LIBOR decide to make it go up. The role of government is to protect its citizens, but it isn't. It's allowing a group of private bankers to get rich on us.

To protect the consumer we should: 1) fix interest rates so customers can anticipate and manage their debt, 2) limit the interest on consumer debt to single digit rates, i.e., not over 9 percent, and 3) separate the commercial banks from the investment or merchant banks because the former has a fiduciary responsibility to its depositors to make safe loans and investments, but investment banks and brokerages by their very nature make more speculative and risky investments that the depositors should not be exposed to. The roles of banks, investment companies and insurance companies need to be divided; they simply have too much power and control over markets and governments to the effect of controlling policy and routinely take advantage of the consumers and taxpayers; privatizing profits and socializing debt.

16

One Person One Vote. I submit that we replace our old Electoral College voting system with a direct vote. All votes can be make electronically, its more efficient, adds transparency, and better represents the will of the people. I submit that every American should have his or her own porthole to government on line, from home or library, where he or she could receive confirmation that his or her vote was counted and gain direct access to current bills under consideration, executive orders, and other government policies, and be able to register concern, hope, or support. This connectivity would allow the citizens to express their sentiments and inform our government of their desires and demands.

All voting requires oversight and protection under the law, and we would need safeguards against government surveillance or hacking, but encryption technology is already used by our Department of Defense and other agencies. A stronger citizen to government relationship leads to a stronger democracy and economy. Presidents could e-mail questions to the whole country, solicit feedback, share ideas, and listen to concerns and complaints (digitally tabulated). Congress could look at responses and get a better feel for the sentiments of the people; if people felt they were being heard, they would get more involved, and that is what is needed for a strong democracy.

17

Monopoly Management. Corporations are growing larger and more powerful than governments, and the control over natural resources, politics, and policies is increasingly more in the hands of a select few and less of the government or of the people. Corporations generally hate government involvement, but thus far every time lobbyists have removed or diminished government protections we have entered into another recession. Each recession or depression can be traced directly to deregulation; greed is at the bottom of it all.

I submit that leaders of industry and the congress should meet publically in forums that are available to the public, to discuss and debate challenges and opportunities openly. Globalization is inevitable, but without government oversight and protection we are all going to be governed by corporate leaders who are not paid to protect the consumer but rather to extract as much money from them from sales as is possible. There are competing interests, and our government needs to represent the people over those of a wealthy few.

We need a court system and a supreme court that represents the interests of the people, over that of the elite. Corporations are not persons; they have no heart or soul, and need to be watched and governed by those representing the people rather than a political party or financial backer. Overturning Glass-Steagall, the Clayton Act, and the Sherman Antitrust act shows the partiality for the politically connected and disregard for the average American; those bills were created for our protection and they worked. What right did they have to take them away without even a public discussion about it? Every citizen should think about this, and these sentiments need to be conveyed to our highest courts and Supreme Court justices. We have to hold them accountable.

18

Blocking a World Currency. Plans are already being made to create a world currency that would diminish the role of the U.S. dollar and compromise the statutes, laws, and will of the American people. It will put control of world money, credit, and banking in the hands of a few, and render our own congress and treasury impotent.

19

Offshore Funds. Corporations and wealthy individuals hold their wealth in offshore accounts to avoid paying taxes, and all those incomes which amount to almost one-third of corporate revenues, should be taxed along with everyone else. Eliminate trusts, why should the rich not have to pay the same taxes as the rest? Why do we have tax laws that consistently protect the wealthy and strip the middle class? Because we let them.

20

Accountability Audits. We need to audit the Federal Reserve; we need to learn where the money is, how it has and is being used, and discuss what is in the best interests of the nation, rather than rely on a few who meet in secret, and have clearly failed in their duties again and again.

Second, we need to audit every senator, president, cabinet member, and congressman after five years of office, whether still in office or not, and five years thereafter until five years after they retire, to ensure that graft and corruption ends. Only if there is accountability and consequences for actions will corruption cease. There needs to be complete transparency for high office. If every representative of the people expected an audit, government and corporate crime would be substantially abated. We need more accountable and ethical leadership, thus we should demand it, and our leaders should expect as much. We ask for noble statesmen like our founding fathers, and if we don't put pressure on our government to end this corruption it won't end, it up to us.

Finally, we need to tax offshore accounts and trusts. The 1 percent get rich while laborers' pensions are destroyed; the wealthiest pay little or no taxes while the middle class get hustled. These problems do not require rocket science; they only require ethical leadership. Enlightened leadership is needed to bring forth the changes needed. We need people who are not in government for personal profit or gain but those whose allegiance is with the people and the constitution rather than an elite cadre that serves its own interests.

21

A National Challenge. Let us commit, say, $10 billion dollars to discover, create, and develop the next 100 best products or services Americans can develop and sell on world markets. We as a people will invest and take ownership in these new companies or projects; we can support American corporations, not with under the table payoffs, but by investing in good ideas that employ people.

We start with a manageable allotment, and observe the effects on employment, productivity, and inflation; if it encourages growth without inflating, we can add a second allotment. If any inflation occurs, we hold off further investment until the economy catches up. The key to a strong economy is to create value through the development of human and natural resources. Creating true value, not just profit, is the key. Watching the growth ourselves, publically, we can all see what needs to be done. Nobody needs to meet in secret; it's all in the open.

Moreover, any dividends paid from these investments will go directly to Social Security for the good of all citizens; new jobs will also add funds back to social security and build a stronger tax base. Moreover, Social Security should from now on be protected from collateralization or withdrawal. The Social Security funds become a cash asset of the United States that shores up the value of our currency; it's a sacred trust and must be protected...from our own government.

Conclusion

Our future, our quality of life, and freedom are dependent on the choices we now have to make. All the world's great spiritual teachers teach us to become more conscious of our own thoughts, words, and actions; to shun money and power; and learn to serve selflessly for the betterment of mankind. It's not about making money; it's about making a difference. You create value by giving something of value; enlightened capitalism is to use money to create the greatest value to the most people in society, to create the most prosperity, happiness and peace for all. Just trying to make as much money as possible has proven again and again to create suffering and pain. We need to enlighten.

This point is epitomized in the classic tale of the devil tempting Jesus Christ in the desert during his meditation as related in Matthew, Mark, and Luke. The devil gives Jesus the final and greatest test when he offers Jesus "All the kingdoms of the earth." All the wealth and power is offered by the devil, but Christ had enlightened and saw the desire for money and power as the devil's trick. We are all being similarly tempted, and every one of us, regardless of our faith, has to decide which master to serve and what path we will take.

God Bless America. May the Whole World Live in Peace.

Resources

Congressional Research Service http://loc.gov/crsinfo/

http://www.historicalstatistics.org/

http://www.bls.gov/fls/#laborforce

http://epic.org/privacy/terrorism/hr3162.html

http://www.archives.gov/federal-register/executive-orders/disposition.html

http://www.whitehouse.gov/briefing-room/presidential-actions/executive-orders

http://www.fas.org/irp/crs/RL31377.pdf

http://www.supremecourt.gov/

http://www.federalreserve.gov/

http://www.fcic.com/

http://www.worldoil.com

http://ideas.repec.org/

http://nep.repec.org/

http://thomas.loc.gov

http://econpapers.repec.org/

http://oll.libertyfund.org

Books

The Federalist Papers by James Madison, Alexander Hamilton and John Jay

Tragedy and Hope: A History of The World in Our Time by Carroll Quigley

The House of Rothschild by Niall Ferguson

Woodrow Wilson's Right Hand, The Life of Colonel Edward M. House by Godfrey Hodgson

Secrets of the Temple, How the Federal Reserve Runs the Country by William Greider

The Creature from Jekyll Island by G. Edward Griffin

The House of Morgan by Ron Chernow

Titan, The Life of John D. Rockefeller by Ron Chernow

The Warburgs by Ron Chernow

Prospect for America, The Rockefeller Panel Reports by the Rockefeller Brothers Fund

The Secret History of the American Empire by John Perkins

The Tyranny of Oil by Antonia Juhasz

A People's History of the United States by Howard Zinn

The Clash of Civilizations and the Remaking of World Order by Samuel P. Huntington

The World is Flat, by Thomas Friedman

Media Control: The Spectacular Achievements of Propaganda by Norm Chompsky

The 9/11 Commission Report Authorized Edition (Congress)

The Royal Families of Europe by Geoffrey Hindley

The Robber Barons by Matthew Josephson

The Secrets of the Federal Reserve by Eustace Mullins

1984 by George Orwell

The New World Order by H.G. Wells

America's Great Depression by Murray Rothbard

The Road to Serfdom by F. A. Hayek

Human Action: A Treatise on Economics by Ludwig von Mises

Capitalism and Freedom by Milton Freedman

International Economics: Theory and Policy by Paul Krugman and Maurice Obstfeld

End the Fed by Ron Paul

Unsafe at Any Speed by Ralph Nader

So, You Wish to Learn All About Economics by Lyndon LaRouche

Bond of Secrecy by Saint John Hunt

Look up everything you question on Wikipedia.com and then YouTube.com. Look at the documentaries available on Netflix. com, look at opposing ideas. Other contrary points of view by Alex Jones can be viewed at www.infowars.com and related Web sites.

Author

Steven S. Sadleir is a best-selling author, consultant and guru. He is director of the Self Awareness Institute based in Laguna Beach, California. For speaking engagements and media or upcoming events contact:

Self Awareness Institute

668 No. Coast Hwy., #417

Laguna Beach, CA 92651

www.SelfAwareness.com

949-355-3249

Other books by Steven

Looking for God: A Seeker's Guide to Religious and Spiritual Groups of the World.

Self Realization: An Owner-User Manual for Human Beings

Christ Enlightened: The Lost Teachings of Jesus Unveiled

The Awakening: An Evolutionary Leap in Human Consciousness

Online, distance learning and teleconferences courses, retreats and seminars with Steven are also available through the Self Awareness Institute and you can sign up for our free newsletter and receive free downloads at www.SelfAwareness.com.